Thinking and Reasoning in Therapy

Thinking and Reasoning in Therapy

Narratives from practice

Susan E. Ryan
Elizabeth Anne McKay

Stanley Thornes (Publishers) Ltd

First published in 1999 by:
Stanley Thornes (Publishers) Ltd
Ellenborough House
Wellington Street
Cheltenham
GL50 1YW
United Kingdom

99 00 01 02 03 / 10 9 8 7 6 5 4 3 2 1

A catalogue record for this book is available from the British Library

ISBN 0 7487 3717 0

Typeset by WestKey Ltd., Falmouth, Cornwall
Printed and bound in Great Britain by T. J. International, Padstow, Cornwall

Contents

SECTION THREE   Interactional and educational applications

FOREWORD

Rosemary Barnitt
School of Occupational Therapy and Physiotherapy, University of Southampton

This book comes at a watershed in occupational therapy, a turning point in the affairs of the profession. This has come about for two reasons: first, the normal developmental pattern of any new professional group and second, the political and economic context in which occupational therapy is practised. In its infancy and early childhood in the 1950s and 1960s occupational therapists were thin on the ground, but their role and skills were well understood by referrers and patients. At that time the professional bodies laid down training content which included macramé, glovemaking, weaving, splinting, physical fitness and ballroom dancing among others, leading purportedly to active bodies and active minds. The profession reached puberty in the 1970s and 1980s, with existential angst about self, bids for independence and concern for being understood by others. The publication of this book comes at the point in the 1990s where adolescence is well developed and therapists are looking back for security to the roots of the profession and looking forward with some impatience to established, recognised and research-based practice.

Professional development has been dependent on societal changes in the 20th century. Occupational therapists have adapted practice to reflect the results of wars, migration, economic booms and recessions, rapid advances in technology and health care, as well as the vagaries of political systems. Regardless of these events, a continuing theme in occupational therapy practice has been the abilities which therapists have developed in process skills when engaging with their clients to achieve a therapeutic relationship and outcome.

To date, much of the literature for occupational therapists about therapeutic processes has been borrowed from other disciplines such as psychology and sociology. However, the profession is now entering its adult years and with this maturity there is a desire to claim territory which belongs legitimately to occupational therapy. The book you are about to read will tell you about process in occupational therapy through the use of narratives or stories. Not only is this central to professional practice, it will also ensure that the book is read. Everyone likes stories and even in preliterate times the storymaker or storyteller was an important member of any society. Today, in every therapy department and staff room, communicating through stories can be observed as the favoured method of social intercourse. Writing a book with or through stories does, however, have one disadvantage. Give a therapist a magazine with diet, fashion, home improvement or gardening articles in it and most will turn promptly to the 'problem' page – real-life stories of disadvantages and dilemma. Give the present book of narratives to therapists and some will find it irresistible to search out the 'stories' without addressing the more difficult theoretical and reflective aspects of each chapter. Cunningly, the editors have addressed this human fallibility by constructing chapters in a number of ways. First, there are brief resumés of content at the start of each chapter and it will be difficult, having glanced at these, not to want to know what happened to Jenny, Angelica and Alison. Second, some chapters have the writer's story running alongside the participant's and third, with few exceptions, the language used in the book is straightforward without over-use of jargon. The individual authors have managed to relate their material to every-one's favourite topic, problem-based learning, creative thinking, discourse analysis and so on. Hopefully, we are now in the decade of the adult therapist, who will appreciate the need for understanding theory and explanation as well as enjoying the stories.

Returning to the original point, the special skill of occupational therapy is work-ing with process rather than content. The book title is *Thinking and Reasoning*, both process skills. For the more reflective reader several happy hours can be spent trying to decide what the difference is between 'thinking' and 'reasoning' and why the book was not entitled *Narratives from Practice*. However, for the reader intent on addressing the current watershed or turning point in the profession, this book is readable, optimistic, rich and feels right. It should help to lead the profession into wise middle age, but watch out for the doomed love affairs, the painful separations and the fear of adult responsibility, all pitfalls on the road to professional maturity.

Contributors

Chris Chapparo DipOT, MA, PhD, OTR, FAOTA
Senior Lecturer, School of Occupational Therapy, University of Sydney, Lidcombe, NSW 2141, Australia

Rachelle Coe BApp Sc (Occupational Therapy)
Senior Occupational therapist, Penrith Community Health Centre, PO Box 94, Penrith, NSW 2751, Australia

Tracy Fortune
Lecturer, Occupational Therapy, School of Community Health, Charles Sturt University, PO Box 789, Albury, NSW 2640, Australia

Mary Jenkins DipCOT, BSc (Hons), PhD
Counsellor, Glenview Park, Strabane, County Tyrone, BT82 8LU, Northern Ireland

Ruth Erica Living
School of Occupational Therapy, St Bartholomew's and the Royal London School of Medicine, Queen Mary and Westfield College, Turner Street, London E1 2AD, England, UK

Alice Lowenstein
Funding Director, Vital Life After Trauma, 53 Linden Street, Brookline, MA 02146, USA

Elizabeth Anne McKay DipCOT, BSc(Hons), MSc
Senior Lecturer, University College of St Martin, Lancaster, England, UK

Matthew Molineux BOccThy, MSc, SROT
Lecturer, Discipline of Occupational Therapy, University College of Ripon and York St John, Lord Mayor's Walk, York YO31 7EX, England, UK

Linda Robertson PhD, Med, BA, NZROT
Senior Lecturer, Otago Polytechnic, Private Bag 1910, Department of Occupational Therapy, Dunedin, New Zealand

Susan E. Ryan BAppSc, MSc
Reader in Educational Development, Department of Health Sciences, University of East London, Romford Road, London, E15 4LZ, England, UK

Sharan L. Schwartzberg EdD, OTR, FAOTA
Professor and Chair, Tufts University, Boston School of Occupational Therapy, Medford, MA 01255, USA

ACKNOWLEDGEMENTS

From Susan

Many people inspired and supported me as I was putting this book together. Working with Elizabeth has been every bit as rewarding as I thought it would be. She has been constructive with her comments on my writing and has worked as a true partner. There are others, though, who have not been so directly involved. I have to thank Sarah Beeston, the Head of Health Sciences at my university, for giving me the freedom that is needed to produce a book. Della Fish is a constant source of inspiration and we have enjoyed numerous dinners debating many of the ideas in this book. Joy Higgs has always given me wise advice and thanks to Dave O'Reilly who always affirms my way of working. Special appreciation goes to the innovative thinking of the postgraduates on the Masters course which I lead. Some past graduates have contributed chapters to this book while others have given me many ideas. Last but not least, no undertaking such as this can come to fruition without personal love and support and this I have received in abundance from my wonderful family Barbara, Helen, David and Tsering and from Paul. Thank you.

From Elizabeth

My thanks go to my family and friends who are always encouraging, enthusiastic and supporting of my endeavours. Special thanks to my parents who so positively supported my career change into occupational therapy all those years ago, a career which has broadened my horizons and offered opportunities beyond my dreams. To colleagues and patients at the Royal Edinburgh Hospital, who provided a challenging and stimulating environment for a 'young' therapist to flourish. They still do. To Sue who offers inspiration and belief. Lastly to the students and educators who willingly share their time, their stories and their knowledge and who never fail to surprise and amaze me.

INTRODUCTION

Narrative is the primary form by which
human experience is made meaningful.

Polkinghorne (1988)

Narrative, that is, the telling of stories, can be considered as giving an account of any occurrence. Throughout history, stories have passed from generation to generation. The stories have educated, entertained, mystified and healed. Whatever the story's message for both the storyteller and the listener, the experience connects them to each other, to their culture, to their past, their present and their possible future. Sharing the story enables people to understand themselves and their world better.

This book presents stories from occupational therapy practice. These stories are told by a range of people: some are told by the therapist involved directly with the client, some are about other therapists and their work, one therapist tells the stories from a multidisciplinary team, another presents the personal perspective of an occupational therapy educator, one deals with students' stories from fieldwork and finally a chapter is told collaboratively by a therapist and a client. What is important is that these stories are told as these narratives reflect a width of practice including both clinical and educational perspectives.

The authors are drawn from the UK, Australia, New Zealand and the United States of America. Each of their stories promotes an individualised account of a specific intervention and each is contextually and culturally bound. These international perspectives give insights into the differing cultural systems, expectations and values. Ethical issues are also highlighted. Emphasis is placed on the therapist's reasoning so that readers can recognise the impact of treatment, the therapist's way of working, the reasoning process and the benefits to the client and practice.

Throughout the book, you will be able to compare other occupational therapists' practice with your own work. In writing the stories, all the authors had an opportunity to reflect directly on their work. As you read the chapters you will be able to reflect on your own practice and the profession. Links to your ways of working and reasoning can be made, comparisons drawn and contrasts highlighted. The stories provide ways of reflecting on your own knowledge and development. Eraut (1994) discussed the importance of knowledge use and knowledge creation for professional development. He argued that knowledge must be codified and made public, that this sharing allows for ordering of the knowledge, which develops cohesion, understanding and, importantly, meaning. Here we attempt to make public the 'processing of therapist's reasoning' by the explicit sharing of stories by experienced therapists and offering explanations of the processes described. By means of the stories provided, we hope to offer examples which facilitate knowledge of the theorising processes, understandings and meanings and the use of current conceptual frameworks.

The stories give an opportunity to view differing research strategies. The use of narrative as a research method is explored and the narratives included illustrate its use as a qualitative methodology aimed at gaining understanding of client, student and therapist perspectives. Such insights can be utilised to alter practice and practitioners. The academic use of narrative to explain practice cannot be overstated. Narrative can provide information in a way which is commonplace to all, thereby allowing dissemination to others. It has an integral role to play in continuing professional education.

We wished this book to be a useful learning tool for you and we wanted you to be able to use the text in a variety of ways. Each chapter presents ways of looking at reasoning and practice. As a result, each opens with key points being presented, which will help you to appreciate those parts of the text. A brief introduction by the editors aims to give further insights into the chapter. Similarly, at the end of each story we suggest further thoughts and questions and put forward exercises which we hope will enable you to understand the theoretical and practical implications of the story. We hope that the text will be used for discussion amongst peers, the content acting as a trigger for further enquiry. Problem- and enquiry-based learning could be stimulated by the chapters as you consider how you would have dealt with the same story.

The book can be a catalyst for you to share your own stories, either retrospectively (clients with whom you have worked) or prospectively (making stories as you work with clients). These stories could provide further vehicles for you to discuss practice. There are a variety of ways in which to compare and contrast practice; for example:

- self
- peer group
- others
  - different staff groups
  - same staff group
  - clients and family
  - associations and organisations which offer services and support.

Whatever you bring to this book through your life experience and your practice as a therapist, each of you will have a unique view of practice. How much you reflect and your preferred ways of reflecting will mean that each of you will generate a range of unique responses. As you progress you may change your responses or you may strengthen your initial thoughts. There are no right or wrong answers. Enjoy the stories, let them challenge and affirm your practice as an occupational therapist.

REFERENCES

Eraut, M. (1994) *Developing Professional Knowledge and Competence*. Falmer Press, London.

Polkinghorne, D.E. (1988) *Narrative Knowing and the Human Sciences*. State University of New York Press, Albany.

1   WHY NARRATIVES?

Susan Ryan

KEY POINTS
- Personal narratives
- Practice complexity
- Narrative reasoning
- Research methods

In this chapter you are introduced to our reasons for compiling this book. We put forward the argument that by using narratives, individual learning and theorising are enriched from the start of professional education, reasoning becomes situated in the personal and the individual and practice becomes contextualised. Rich narratives tell about the uncertainties of life. This assists learners to delve into the complex issues that they will encounter at work. They show a different picture from the usual ways of presenting material. Narratives told by experienced therapists can illuminate the intricacies and subtle nuances of particular ways of working and the reader can construct ideas from them and take them from the particular into the general sphere of their own work. These ideas can then be adjusted and applied in similar circumstances even though not always in the same form. Although narratives were originally used in other disciplines they were introduced into occupational therapy at the end of the 1980s by Cheryl Mattingly's doctoral study examining the clinical reasoning abilities of therapists. They offer an interesting alternative.

> *Study the science of art and the art of science.*
> *Learn to see and remember that everything is connected to everything else.*
> Leonardo da Vinci

As you read this book it will become part of your personal narrative just as it is part of ours. It marks another step along a fascinating learning road we the editors, Elizabeth McKay and Susan Ryan, are following. Elizabeth and I work in undergraduate and postgraduate occupational therapy courses and over the past years we have become convinced that narratives offer a perspective of practice that cannot be ignored. They can include rich detail that is often excluded from other procedural or scientific accounts of practice. They highlight the complexities of life situations that an occupational therapist has to consider and reason through. This way of examining practice underpins much of everyday work as we continually listen to, tell and make stories as well as reflect on and then revise them.

In this chapter we have tried to take you on a journey from general thoughts about narratives through to the specifics of learning and reasoning. In the following sections we would like to tell the story of how the book was written.

WHY THIS BOOK?

This book is a collection of narratives told by experienced occupational therapists, both clinicians and educators. As both of us work with aspects of clinical reasoning, we felt that this book was a natural progression to our work and presents practice in a different light. We wanted to respond to criticisms about professionals and their education that have been voiced by Eraut (1994). We chose narratives as our contribution because they fill in some of the gaps which he has identified.

WHAT WE ASKED THE AUTHORS TO DO

When we approached the contributors they were all happy to be part of this book but it was interesting to see the reactions of some to our request for stories about practice. Although they were all experienced therapists, some had been so well schooled in the scientific, positivistic way of thinking and academic writing that they had great trouble changing their style. We sent them samples from the work of the world-renowned neurologist Oliver Sacks. We asked them to talk to you as they wrote yet use the literature to support their claims. It was more difficult for some than others.

What we wanted was a variety of narratives from different settings as well as a spectrum of practice that reflected both hospital, differing community work and education, both fieldwork and academic. By asking therapists from several countries to write about their work, we hoped to provide an avenue whereby you could compare their practice with that in your country. In this way you are able to look at a wider picture of health care, the status of the profession, the cultural beliefs and the knowledge and confidence of the patients or clients who are part of the story.

We did not specify how we wanted them to use the story form and because of this we received a rich variety of methods illustrating different ways of using narratives. These you can use as a template or a guide. There are also strong themes emerging from this collection. Running through all the accounts is the individual interpretation of practice as well as the sensitivity towards a particular way of working. This is coupled with knowledge from clinical reasoning studies and reflection, which all the authors are familiar with in varying degrees, which is why they were asked to contribute. We hope their accounts will spark ideas so that new forms of work emerge for you and for the profession. We think the following quote sums up the essence of our beliefs:

Each man builds up his own world of clinical experience and assumes personal, that is, virtually individual, responsibility for the way he manages cases in that world.

Friedson (1971)

HOW WE ORGANISED THE BOOK

We have used the historical evolution of studies in clinical reasoning, described below, as a broad framework for the placement of the chapters. The stories that come first in Chapters 2 and 3 focus on aspects from the cognitive science, problem-solving and decision-making schools of thought. Chapters 4 to 7 use narratives as the primary tool for describing their work. Chapters 8, 9 and 10 focus on interactional and educational ways of applying some of this work.

You can read all the accounts or dip into ones that interest you. This will depend on your reasons for reading this book and whether these centre on learning more about practice, understanding different ways of reasoning, thinking about ideas for research methodologies or creating innovative educational sessions. Below is a snap-shot account of how clinical reasoning studies have developed in the last three decades and giving an idea of how this knowledge is being applied at present.

A HISTORICAL OVERVIEW OF CLINICAL REASONING STUDIES

At the end of the 1960s several events were happening affecting medical education in particular. As medical research escalated there was an unprecedented explosion of knowledge. Some medical educators realised that it was not possible to fit all this new material into a curriculum. They felt that there must be other ways for their students to assimilate the material in their courses and, indeed, to continue learning beyond their graduation. These realisations prompted interest in ways of facilitating the concept of lifelong learning. Because of these ideas, some research studies started focusing on how students and experts reason in order to understand better the processes that occur as professional experience develops.

It was also in this era that computer technology was becoming more widely available and was having an impact on other areas. This created a knowledge field about storing and retrieving information. So many of the first clinical reasoning studies looked at the cognitive aspects of the human mind and in particular how memory functioned. These studies were scientific and precise; they focused on hierarchical and procedural aspects of knowledge retention and retrieval. Although they were not named as such until the close of the 1980s, they formed the school of thought called cognitive science.

Another scientific group, called the decision-making school, was realising that humans had severe biases in processing information. They tried to study reasoning and expose and eliminate any personal bias from thinking. This became so precise that mathematical formulae were sometimes used to calculate decisions and algorithm trees tracing all the eventualities of decisions were designed. These focused entirely on the procedural, medical aspects of reasoning.

The third major group stemmed from the discipline of psychology and was called the concept-learning school. Here researchers studied how concepts were formed and layered in a person's mind and how each person differed in their perception of information. Knowledge was 'chunked' according to associations from a person's past experiences.

All these groups started looking at new ways for educators to present material. Research methods comparing expert and novice reasoning about similar situations were studied and the essential differences were teased out so that the development and stages of knowledge formation were understood better.

During this period from the early 1970s to the 1980s allied work was happening with other forms of learning for adults who had not accessed higher education before. Theories about adult learning or andragogy were put forward and contrasted with pedagogical approaches used with children. Another focus centred on reflection and its use in learning. No theories were put forward but the actual use of reflection was studied, certain techniques were created and some models were published. It was during the last decade that the reflective works of Boud, Keogh and Walker (1985), Boud and Walker (1991), Fish, Twinn and Purr (1991), Mezirow (1991) and Schon (1983, 1987) also started appearing. These sat alongside the newly developing theories about adult learning discussed above and together they acknowledged personal experiences and interpretations, which was in contrast to the purely scientific approaches. All this work was happening within a change in broader scientific thinking.

These changes coincided with the end of the modernist viewpoint, which had dominated thought for 200 years. The post-modernist era was ushered in and these new ways of thinking started appearing in the literature and different interpretations of a phenomenon were accepted.

It was during this period that the American study of the clinical reasoning of occupational therapists in a physical rehabilitation setting in Boston took place. Occupational therapy in the USA was changing so the American Occupational Therapy Association and the American Occupational Therapy Foundation commissioned this research. The two researchers involved in this study came from different disciplines. The original investigator of practice was Cheryl Mattingly, an anthropologist. Her PhD supervisor was Professor Donald Schon who was writing about reflection. Thus the study had a social science orientation as well as a reflective input. Maureen Fleming was an occupational therapy educator who joined the study after the first year. Her work touched upon, but was different from, the earlier medical reasoning studies although stylistically some parts of her work were similar. This study heralded new ways of talking about the people we work with and new words were brought in to the professional language. It also supported and encouraged other writers who had started using qualitative research methods in occupational therapy.

Mattingly's work brought in the use of narratives in different ways; she introduced the phenomenological perspective that considered the meaning of the illness experience for the person in therapy. In essence, this study was a fertilisation across disciplines. We felt that these other methods were more appropriate to describe and as a means of understanding much of the work that occupational therapists do. Let us stop for one moment and consider the main features of narratives and narrative reasoning as Mattingly explains them. Later in the chapter we will examine her actual findings.

NARRATIVE REASONING

The original thinking about narrative reasoning is described in detail in Chapter 10 of Mattingly and Fleming's (1994) book. Essentially, there is an enormous shift from describing and thinking about practice through medical, technical rational or procedural terms. This is because, as was stated earlier, this way of talking came from another discipline, the social sciences. As narratives are temporal, practice, described thus, includes a larger holistic picture of a person. It situates their therapeutic intervention as only a tiny part of a life story that has been disrupted by an unforeseen event. A person's past experiences, their values, roles and habits are viewed as chapters. Interventions and prospective stories make up an unfolding text that often is not smooth. Using narrative reasoning a therapist will try to enter into that person's story so that their personal meanings about life become embedded in the therapeutic event and, as Mattingly describes, the actors become players in the developing story. Talking about a man with head injuries, she says, 'The therapeutic time together itself had to provide a kind of existential picture of how he might live his life in the future with his disability' (p. 245). An interesting distinction between biomedical time and narrative time is that it is actor centred rather than disease centred. The disease merely adds some understanding to what is happening. The main character is the person with the pathology (Sacks, 1985).

Mattingly points out that in so many applications of therapy there is no narrative, no plot, only an intervention as therapists struggle to talk the language of medicine. Another feature of narrative reasoning is the use of emplotment that comes from the language of literature. According to Mattingly, there are five features associated with the story that is played out between the therapist and the patient:

1 action and motive which are key structuring devices;
2 narrative time is organised within a gap, a place of desire where one wants to be;
3 narratives show how things and people change over time and that this is full of tricks and reversals;
4 narrative time is dramatic and conflict is often present with obstacles to be overcome;
5 endings are uncertain and so narrative time is marked by suspense (Mattingly and Fleming (1994), pp. 253, 254).

From this brief overview you can see, as Mattingly writes, that narrative thinking is central in providing therapists with a way to consider disability in the phenomenological terms of injured lives (p. 268). It is powerful for many reasons.

AFTER MATTINGLY

From 1988 onwards there has been a proliferation and a great interest in both the study of clinical reasoning and the methods used to examine it. Many recent papers are applying this knowledge to practice and education. Recently, Neistadt (1998) has studied the effects of using a narrative framework with students by asking them to write one or two paragraphs about a person's story and a foreseen ending. Their stories speak volumes about their thinking (p. 225). It should be said that the introduction of narratives has also caused great confusion as some people continue to work and think in the scientific or positivistic way. The two different methods are often applied without understanding where they came from so it is essential to comprehend how these roots are manifested (Ryan, 1998). We hope this book will contribute to this exploration.

Susan was in New York when the clinical reasoning study was being conducted. She altered her dissertation focus so that she could study clinical reasoning. Her work was assessed by Deborah Yarret-Slater who was the head occupational therapist in the Boston study. In the 1990s Elizabeth studied and then worked with Susan on narrative aspects of clinical reasoning in mental health, as you can see in her chapter about Lillian.

Now, having set both the clinical reasoning and the occupational therapy scene to some extent, we would like to take you back to look at the use of narratives in a general sense.

NARRATIVES AND STORIES

If you look up definitions of narratives and stories you will find that the former are sometimes referred to as a story whereas this does not happen the other way around (*New Oxford Dictionary of English*, 1998). Stories, according to this source, are more entertaining whereas narratives appear to be more serious. This is a fine distinction and one that is not upheld in many articles or even in this book but it is worth bearing in mind as the words are used interchangeably.

We are all exposed to tales from our earliest memories. Writing about childhood stories, the developmental psychologist Susan Engel (1994) believes they go far beyond their immediate charm. They have such an effect that both the stories we hear and those that we tell shape who we are. She writes, 'They give body to our experience and take us beyond the confines of everyday life into the past, the future, the might be' (p. vii). Perhaps this is the key to their use in undergraduate programmes as they will be remembered more clearly and for far longer than factual things alone, as Matthew Molineux's chapter reveals. From times immemorial, narratives have been a way of passing on oral traditions to succeeding generations. Perhaps it is this familiarity which engages the therapists and students we have worked with. Perhaps it is because of the insights and possibilities that are suddenly generated. We believe it is more than this. As we shall see, we think it is a reaction to the way practice has been presented previously.

Occupational therapists have, in the past, tried to present themselves as being part of a scientific, medically oriented profession. The way of thinking and talking about practice has followed the reductionist, logical approach used by researchers in the natural sciences and medicine has followed this way of reasoning as well, although this is changing in many medical courses. Stories from and about practice seem to breathe life, human life, into the drier aspects of our work which come from rational, so-called 'left brain' thinking. This is described by Peter Senge (1996) when he writes about what he calls this 'left brain bias':

> *From an early age, we are taught to break apart problems, to fragment the world. This apparently makes complex tasks and subjects more manageable. But we pay a hidden enormous price: we can no longer see the consequences of our actions. We lose our intrinsic sense of connection to a larger whole. (p. 17).*

This 'larger whole' is the part of practice that includes the person's feelings, the way they perceive their situation, their reactions to that particular situation, the way you react to them and many other highly personal facets. Unless we are talking only about the technical aspects of our work, everything else involves people. Alice Lowenstein, in her joint chapter with Sharan Schwartzberg, writes movingly about her changing perceptions and needs over a long period of recovery from a head injury that spanned several years. From this account alone, we can see that our work and her needs are not simple or logical whereas some of the procedural and technical aspects of therapy can appear to be.

As we read the quotation above, we can all think of practice situations that cannot be reduced to parts. Occupational therapy, when it is carried out in complex situations, is often concerned with working with people over long periods of time. Our process of working cannot be reduced to a linear sequence except in straightforward work. Rachelle Coe's chapter shows the twists, turns and foldings back that happened to her as she worked with Jenny.

Even at postgraduate level, we have found therapists wishing to have a 'correct, uncomplicated answer'. This could be a result of their undergraduate learning experiences as knowledge about clinical reasoning has only recently become a subject on some courses and may not be fully integrated into courses overall. Furthermore, it also depends on which school of thought the reasoning is embracing. At times, therapists who think simplistically like this do not seem to be able to cope with complexity and the messiness of actual practice that Fish (1995) and Schon (1983, 1987) describe in their writings on reflection. It appears to be non-scientific, which in actual fact it is.

In contrast to the situation described above, some creative students who are comfortable with the uncertainty of work are limited, once they graduate, by therapists who work in the more rigid manner described above. It appears that two things can happen to these new therapists. They either start to practise in a routine and mechanical way and then lose interest in the profession and leave or they decide to perfect and then bury these routines into their subconscious. At this juncture they often change jobs. Having converted their technical knowledge into hidden, tacit knowledge, they then feel free to concentrate on illuminating other aspects of practice. It is the latter situation that creates a therapist described by Fish (1995) as a practical artist. We agree with Fish who argues that embracing uncertainty and working artistically should happen from the start of professional education rather than by chance later. Much depends on the way in which the educational experiences are presented.

This is where narratives have such an important part to play. Some theories of learning development suggest that new learners are not able to incorporate other elements into their thinking. Elizabeth's experience with her student on fieldwork, which we shall relate later in this chapter, showed that they could. So there appear to be issues around how people are taught at undergraduate and postgraduate levels as well as how practising therapists think about and articulate their practice.

This argument brings in another dimension found in narratives or other forms of rich description and that is how we make sense of multifaceted information. Coming from psychology, Gelb (1996) thinks the priority should be centred on how therapists view their problem solving. He states that it is more important to have the ability to ask the right question(s) in the first place. He thinks that valuable time is lost sorting through complex data looking for outcomes when more emphasis should be placed on the initial sorting-through period. It is crucial to be able to sift out or perhaps even to redefine a situation from the mass of material a therapist is presented with. This indicates the point from which to start working. This ability is not acquired easily, as it is a highly attuned skill that underlies wise professional judgement. If the starting point is too simple then students do not develop this skill or they actually expect practice to be simple. Linda Robertson's chapter centres on this way of looking at problems.

All the narratives in this book can be questioned, discussed and challenged but their narrative format gives a connection and a 'wholeness' to situations. The adult educationalist Mezirow (1991) writes that, 'The narrative form groups related ideas to give coherence to the story being told rather than categorising characteristics that are somehow similar' (p. 146).

Another important reason why we wanted to present narratives to you is that it gives us a voice. Narrative seems to make it possible to capture the attention of people who normally would not have the patience to listen. One striking example of this came from Jeanne, a postgraduate physiotherapist at Susan's university. She worked with young people using procedures that were extremely painful. She was concerned about several areas of this practice but it was only when she told the harrowing story of one of her patients that the other disciplines reacted. This account caused them to make more careful considerations with the protocols that the department followed. These changes did not lessen the actual trauma but they did make others more aware of the feelings of everyone involved and so Jeanne was listened to and several aspects of this care were altered as a result. So it can be seen that narratives can have a powerful change effect and this is why they have been used therapeutically, as the following section considers.

THE APPEARANCE OF NARRATIVES IN THERAPY

Narratives can be traced back to ancient times and, according to Ricouer (1984), narrative enquiry methods were used by Aristotle and Augustine. In the Middle Ages even Shakespeare's son-in-law John Hall, described by Joseph (1993) as, 'that man, "most excellent in the art" of medicine' (p. 1), wrote detailed stories about his patients. These methods were changed in the 18th century when classificatory rules about diseases dominated medical theory and practice and the person was merely incidental.

According to the French philosopher and historian Michel Foucault (1973), this separation of man from his disease held sway until the 1980s when other forms of literature started to appear. He describes the scientific way like this:

In order to be able to offer each of our patients a course of treatment perfectly adapted to his illness and to himself, we try to obtain a complete, objective idea of his case; we gather together in a file of his own all the information we have about him. We 'observe' him in the same way that we observe the stars or a laboratory experiment. (p. xv)

In this century many other disciplines have used narratives in different forms. Dewey's work in education covered time, space, experience and sociality as central to these themes (Connelly and Clandinin, 1990). Narrative has been used in history, the philosophy of history, anthropology and the social sciences.

In the therapeutic field the psychotherapists were one of the first to use narrative and the psychologist Carl Rogers wrote in this way in his client-centred work. More general writing from psychology and the human sciences started proliferating in the 1980s. Oliver Sacks (1995), a clinical professor of neurology, started writing fascinating tales about the people he worked with who had neurological diseases. His way of writing was described on the cover of one of his books thus: 'He conducts one to other modes of being which – however abnormal they may be to our way of thinking – may develop virtues and beauties of their own'.

HOW ARE NARRATIVES BEING USED?

From reading the previous sections, you will have a flavour of how narratives are being used. For instance, a developmental psychologist might be interested to examine the structure and cohesiveness of a story. A clinical psychologist might like to see what the stories reveal about a person's emotions. Sometimes the process of the telling is looked at in detail. Ruth Living's chapter presents a multidisciplinary team's stories about one client. This account shows two types of narrative use. Each team member told their story to Ruth and from these she has written a narrative to try to weave the different perspectives together. This form would be interesting to use with crosscultural studies. The teller of the story may also experience an emotional release in the telling. They may develop insights that they had not previously been aware of. Sometimes the opposite may happen and the narrator may become distressed. For this reason the researcher or educator must be prepared to provide support, which is something that ethics committees look for in research proposals.

Narrative enquiry research is being undertaken more often in practice. According to Joy Goodfellow (1997), it can be used to look at experts, to examine practice reflectively and to study the metaphors and naturalistic approaches that are used in evaluation. Essentially, the concern is with embodied experiential knowledge rather than technical conceptual knowledge. Primary accounts can be synthesised and configured into secondary narratives that become a resource for shared meaning. On the other hand, they may be analysed into themes which are peculiar to an individual or which are common across several persons. This work is fluid and there is no 'right way', which makes it a challenge for all of us wanting to study in this way. It is still too soon to be more specific and we have to cope with this messiness even though we aim to be as rigorous as possible.

In practice, many therapists and doctors are moving away from the structured interviews and checklists that were previously used and are allowing their clients to tell their story first. Even though the accounts may differ with each telling, it gives everybody a chance to reflect and retell and by doing this other insights develop into the experiences that are told. In fact, this is the approach for a new form of therapy called narrative therapy that some occupational therapists and others have started using.

Cheryl Mattingly, the anthropologist whose work we described earlier, realised that the occupational therapists she worked with in her study used what she termed narrative framing. They placed these therapy episodes into the much larger narrative of the person's past life and they were able to work with the person with a view of many future possibilities. Even during routine procedural tasks such as balancing on a balance board, the experienced therapist took the opportunity to discuss future work possibilities. She was trying to help the person to gain insight into their condition so that they would realise just how much this could affect their job. It introduced the possibility of other ways of working without saying so directly.

Reasoning in this way helped the therapists to tell stories to their colleagues that either affirmed ideas for their interventions or showed where the gaps and inconsistencies were. This way of working also allows a therapist to get to know their clients more intimately so that even the dialogue with a person is particular. An example of this knowledge is illustrated in Mary Jenkins' chapter where the therapist works on equal terms with her patient.

Narratives can be used in other ways which can be great fun. A story can guide practice where everyone joins in as if it was a real event. At the Australian Pacific Rim Conference in 1995, Cheryl Mattingly gave an account of this way of working in one of the keynote addresses. She told how a young girl who needed to achieve greater range of motion and endurance pretended she was an Olympic athlete. The room was set up and the therapist became her coach. Targets were worked out and the session was like a competition although she was competing only against herself. In the end the therapeutic goal was achieved with a great deal of laughter and pleasure.

Stories can help in other ways. Increasingly it is being realised that experienced therapists have a range of practice knowledges that is hidden (Higgs and Titchen, in press). Apart from the intimate understanding they have of the technical aspects of practice, what is referred to in the clinical reasoning literature as their propositional knowledge, these therapists have developed an artistic and creative way of working that seems 'right' for the individual and the place. This is evidenced by the way they focus on the person's needs, the subtle way they communicate or the manner in which they place the present situation into a wider future perspective. It may be the way they incorporate formal theory into their work or use their own personal theories to elaborate on certain methods.

Whatever it is, it is often not expressed well to those who do not understand what we do. We have found that narratives are vehicles that convey these tacit dimensions. They seem to have properties that transcend disciplines or levels of knowledge, so that everyone takes away new ideas and something that is meaningful. There seems to be some connectedness with our personal world.

How have Elizabeth and Susan used narratives?

Both of us have had many instances where we have been able to deepen another's understanding by incorporating narratives into their learning. It should also be said that our own knowledge and awareness grow each time this happens and often we have insights or see things and connections in other ways.

For example, Elizabeth visited a student on her second fieldwork placement (McKay and Ryan, 1995). This student was trying to describe her work with a lady who had arthritis. She was fitting her description into a presentation formula she believed was 'professional'. This was a procedural way of talking which followed the linear occupational therapy process that is still presented in some undergraduate courses. She was also trying to get it 'right'. In her account the human element was missing, the personal appreciation was not even considered and the focus was on the present. Elizabeth discontinued this line of formal enquiry and started using a narrative approach in her questioning. She learned that the student had a brother with a similar condition and because of this she was familiar with the problems that a family encounters. The richness of detail that followed this switch of styles was remarkable and more meaningful to the student, her supervisor and Elizabeth. It also transcended the stage of procedural learning that the student was at because it incorporated personal life details as well as professional ones. She saw a bigger picture.

Susan has held clinical reasoning workshops for academic and fieldwork educators in many countries. She usually presents the spectrum of studies that have been carried out in the last three decades so that the participants realise what the different types of reasoning are, where they come from and who uses them. She has always been surprised at the eagerness with which narratives have been accepted, even in those countries that pride themselves on being very scientific. The narratives appeared to have quite a revelatory effect on those attending, so much so that the practical exercises which the lecturers designed during the workshop focused mainly on different ways of using narratives with their students.

Cath, a newly qualified therapist who is taking part in Susan's current research into early practice, told about attending a three-day workshop on narratives run by a psychologist. It had a tremendous impact on her and even though she had followed a problem-based learning curriculum that focused on individuals, she had never come across this way of presenting material. In her words, 'It captured our imagination, it's all caught up with the person and their life story'. Its use seems to draw everyone into the picture so that the narrator also becomes included. It seems to release a creative train of thought that has the possibility to transform the way we work.

Students have also responded enthusiastically to the many different ways we have used narratives in sessions at our respective universities. We continue to experiment with these methods and to be intrigued by their results. This book uses narratives in so many ways that any number of ideas can be utilised.

WHAT HAPPENS WHEN WE REASON THROUGH NARRATIVES?

A great deal has been written about the generation of knowledge, how we organise it and make sense from it. Theories about learning come from different roots in the same way as we discussed previously, with the distinctions between the natural sciences, the human sciences and the social sciences. In medical and therapy education there is debate about the most effective learning approaches. Occupational therapy education embraces biomedical and psychosocial knowledge that is increasingly being set within cultural and contextual frameworks. Many of the treatment interventions have specific approaches: for instance, neurodevelopment, motor relearning or the biomechanical approach. These need to be set within wider models of thinking about the person, their family, the community, the larger state and even the national policies. This means that the approach should be considered as only a part of the whole knowledge that is needed.

Learning comes from many disparate and sometimes disconnected sources. How this information is 'put together' depends on the ways the educators present and assess the material they use. Often this assimilation is a painful process for the learners. On one hand, the learners may experience rather personal shifts in their attitudes and this is often termed reorientation. In fact, this should happen if they transform their thinking to higher levels of understanding. However, on top of this, if learning is so diverse and disparate, it is hard to pull it all together and make sense of everything. It causes confusion, extra effort and it takes longer to synthesise all the pieces into a whole.

Because of these issues, there is a great deal of dissatisfaction with professional education and as we said before, it is coming under criticism. One of the most outspoken critics is Professor Michael Eraut (1994) of the University of Sussex, England, who outlines major deficiencies in current practice. Briefly, he believes the problems are twofold. First, professions follow certain systems of thought from one generation to the next in an unquestioning way. According to him, this hinders the development of ways of thinking that are more educationally constructive (p. 49). This echoes what we have said earlier about the positivistic view of practice that was followed, particularly in occupational therapy in the USA, but which is now changing towards the phenomenological view, although at present the views are still mixed and unclear. Second, Eraut says that to make use of different concepts and ideas requires intellectual effort as well as an encouraging work context. He thinks that in the 'busyness' of practice, no model is used that shows ways of working with ideas or concepts. So the theoretical work studied at university is not seen to be of use in practice. Therapists just 'do'!

Educationalists have been addressing these problems. Several ways of putting knowledge together have been tried and problem-based learning (PBL) is one. The advocates of PBL claim a new approach. Rather than studying subjects separately and then synthesising and integrating them later, students working in groups are introduced to problem triggers. These focus on a person with a problem and the group decides what knowledge needs to be learned. There are several stages to this inductive process.

The theory behind this approach is that learning is realistic, it is centred on a human need, it is inductive because it uses an enquiry method to obtain information, it is an active form of learning and so it is supposedly more constructive. It also incorporates personal experience. But, like many other methods, it has its drawbacks although these are, admittedly, in the method of the actual delivery rather than in the idea. Cath, the newly qualified therapist we talked about earlier in connection with a workshop on narratives, had only learned procedural therapy and had not even heard of narratives throughout her three years of tertiary education.

Problem-based learning is not the only way in which a holistic picture can be built up. Some schools are using group reflection in an enquiry-based learning (EBL) way that incorporates real experience as well. Here, time is spent with real people in the community; the educators are from both the academic and the community settings; peer learning and comparative practice take place. Exciting results are emerging. This method, used in Canada and New Zealand, has broken with tradition in the timing of semesters; these elongated modules often span two semesters or one academic year. Learning and experience move between real contexts and the university and are co-facilitated by academics and clinicians. Much reflective work takes place, skills can be practised in a safe environment and questions and discussions occur between all involved. In order to give time for this process to happen, much content work is sacrificed but it has been deemed to be worthwhile as the clinical reasoning abilities of the students become more meaningful.

The main idea with these methods is one of wholeness in thinking. Knowles (1990) writes that, 'This must not come from arbitrary, meaningless parts to meaningful wholes, but instead from simplified wholes to more complex wholes' (p. 67). In this way the learner constructs their knowledge and builds on it. You can see that narratives sit very well with these methods. And because this way of learning draws on human experiences that are actually lived through, the expectations and the consequent learning are more realistic and meaningful. Less 'unlearning' has to occur once a student becomes a therapist. Theory is truly incorporated into practice.

This does not mean that we are specifically advocating PBL or EBL, although they are interesting methods, they are not the only ways to achieve the ends we are discussing here. Recently, more authors such as Manley (1991), Mezirow (1991) and Fish and Coles (1998) are talking about *praxis*, a term used to describe knowledge at a personal level – knowledge that informs action. It arises from practice itself and consequently different ways of using the knowledge from fieldwork are being looked at. Tracy Fortune's chapter deals with some of these ideas.

We are advocating the use of narratives with all this work. In the first instance, a new student will learn to develop their narrative voice, they will understand about 'the gaze' on which their story focuses, and in the second instance, narratives from experienced therapists can be used to trigger, augment, enliven and compare practice. Narratives would work particularly well with the EBL and the reflective methods described earlier. Eraut says emphatically that practical knowledge, particularly of ill-defined problems, spoken about by experienced therapists must be made explicit. They will show their own style, their personal stance and they can augment their narrative of practice with additional commentary. 'Resources of this kind are rarely put at the disposal of professionals in either initial or continuing education' (p. 50). That is the purpose of this book.

We also think narratives could have another purpose in learning. They are so rich in their detail that they can encourage the student to develop their personal theories about practice from the beginning of their education. We have said that stories are familiar, they become alive and students can delve into them and, with help, they can see the large picture as well as the minutiae. Manley (1991) refers to this as first-level theory building that is often missed out of learning experiences. Fish and Coles (1998) illustrate in detail how this personal theory focus may start from an incident within a story. Usually theoretical work starts with second-level theories derived from others which students are encouraged to learn and follow. If they only learn in this way, they either do not form their own theories until much later or they continue to work in a technical rational way within rules and boundaries prescribed by others.

If we look at stories of practice such as the ones in this book, the personal way of working comes over strongly. So, too, does the realisation that the contributors are aware of both the parts and the whole in a constant iteration and reiteration. We think that learners must develop this ability to integrate the large vision with exquisite attention to detail, so that patterns may be nurtured and emerge from the whole even while engaging in immediate actions. This ability uses divergent and convergent thinking, intuition, imagination, creativity and synthesis. Gelb (1996) refers to this as *synvergent thinking*. It is a different model from other patterns of reasoning yet it seems particularly suited to complex situations described in occupational therapy practice. It matches the concept of narrative framing. Narratives are a vehicle that could be used to encourage this development. We hope you will find this so too!

REFERENCES

Boud, D., Walker, D. (1991) In the midst of experience: developing a model to aid learners and facilitators. Paper presented at the National Conference on Experiential Learning,

'Empowerment through Experiential Learning: Explorations of Good Practice'. University of Surrey, 16–18 July.

Boud, D., Keogh, R., Walker, D. (1985) Promoting reflection in learning: a model. In D. Boud. R. Keogh and D. Walker (eds) *Reflection: Turning Experience into Learning*. Kogan Page, London.

Connelly, F., Clandinin, D. (1990) Stories of experience and narrative enquiry. *Educational Researcher*, 19(5), 2–14.

Engel, S. (1994) *The Stories Children Tell. Making Sense of the Narratives of Childhood*. W. H. Freeman, New York.

Eraut, M. (1994) *Developing Professional Knowledge and Competence*. Falmer Press, London.

Fish, D. (1995) *Quality Mentoring for Student Teachers: A Principled Approach to Practice*. David Fulton, London.

Fish, D., Coles C. (1998) *Developing Professional Judgement in Health Care*. Butterworth Heinemann, Oxford.

Fish, D., Twinn, S., Purr, B. (1991) *Promoting Reflection: Improving the Supervision of Practice in Health Visiting and Initial Teacher Training*. West London Institute, London.

Foucault, M. (1973) *The Birth of the Clinic: An Archaeology of Medical Perception*. Tavistock, London.

Gelb, M. (1996) *Thinking for a Change*. Aurum Press, London.

Goodfellow, J. (1997) Analysing data in narrative enquiry. In J. Higgs (ed.) *Writing Qualitative Research*. Hampden Press, Sydney.

Higgs, J., Titchen, A. (in press) *Knowledge for Practice: Knowing, Doing, Being, Becoming*. Hampden Press, Sydney.

Joseph, H. (1993) *Shakespeare's Son-in-law. John Hall: Man and Physician*, 4th edn. Printed in the United States of America.

Knowles, M. (1990) *The Adult Learner*, 4th edn. Gulf, Houston.

Manley, K. (1991) Knowledge from nursing practice. In A. Perry and M. Jolley, (eds) *A Knowledge Base for Practice*. Edward Arnold, London.

Mattingly, C., Fleming, M. (1994) *Clinical Reasoning: Forms of Inquiry in a Therapeutic Practice*. F. A. Davis, Philadelphia.

McKay, E., Ryan, S. (1995) Clinical reasoning through story telling: examining a student's case story on a fieldwork placement. *British Journal of Occupational Therapy*, 58(6), 234–238.

Mezirow, J. (1991) *The Transformative Dimensions of Adult Learning*. Jossey-Bass, San Francisco.

Neistadt, M. (1998) Teaching clinical reasoning as a thinking frame. *American Journal of Occupational Therapy*, 52(3), 221–229.

Ricouer, P. (1984) *Time and Narrative, Vol. 1*. University of Chicago Press, Chicago.

Ryan, S. (1998) Influences that shape our reasoning. In J. Creek (ed.) *The Theory and Philosophy of Occupational Therapy*. Whurr, London.

Sacks, O. (1985) *The Man Who Mistook His Wife for a Hat*. Pan Books Ltd., London.

Sacks, O. (1995) *An Anthropologist on Mars: Seven Paradoxical Tales*. Picador, London.

Schon, D. (1983) *The Reflective Practitioner*. Basic Books, New York.

Schon, D. (1987) *Educating the Reflective Practitioner*. Jossey-Bass, London.

Senge, P. (1996) The fifth discipline: The art and practice of the learning organisation. In M. Gelb (ed.) *Thinking for a Change*. Aurum Press, London.

COGNITIVE SCIENCE, PROBLEM SOLVING AND DECISION MAKING

2 ASSESSING MABEL AT HOME: A COMPLEX PROBLEM-SOLVING PROCESS

Linda Robertson

KEY POINTS
- Hypothesis generation
- Problem identifications and solutions
- Novice and expert differences
- Cues acquisition and pattern recognition

Here problem solving is considered both as an everyday occurrence as well as being, in this instance, specific to occupational therapy practice. The processes of problem identification and solution are critically reviewed and the author highlights where possible errors occur. The myriad facets which influence a therapist's decision making are presented as a pathway of discovery in a seemingly routine home visit.

We are all familiar with problem solving. From childhood onward we actively solve problems that our world presents to us. Last month, for instance, our neighbour had a problem. Her property was flooding near the front door and she claimed that the drainpipe on our property was the culprit as it was leaking and causing water to collect near her house. This is an example of a problem where the general nature of the outcome is known before the situation is fully determined. There could be no doubt that the neighbour wanted the waterlogged ground dried out!

In occupational therapy, many of the problems we deal with are of this type. Consider an elderly man who is afraid of falling when climbing the steps at his front door. In this situation the general outcome is to ensure he feels safe when accessing his house, but until the situation is further defined the method of achieving this is unknown. Maybe a rail would suffice, perhaps the height of the steps needs adjusting, possibly a ramp would be the best solution? The scenario I will discuss later in this chapter is typical of this type of problem where the general nature of the outcome is known but the solutions are yet to be determined.

By contrast, the outcome may be open to interpretation such as a situation where an older person is living alone but is thought by her doctor and her family to be unsafe. A wide range of possibilities exist for the outcome: moving into a rest home, providing home assistance, calling a dietician in as her nutrition is in question, living with a family member, attending a day centre, and hiring out her spare room to a 'companion'. The perception of the problem is crucial to the solution that will be considered. In this case, one occupational therapist's solution may not be the same as another's. One of the characteristics of an ill-defined problem is that there is often a lack of consensus, even by the experts, about what the appropriate solution is.

Essentially, then, a problem is a situation where you are trying to reach some goal and you must find a means to achieve it. There will always be a beginning, a stimulus that provokes an initial response to a particular situation, and a goal which may or may not be well defined at the outset. To solve the problem you must do something that will impact on the initial situation with a view to achieving the goal. Often rules exist that specify allowable operations and these are generally called 'constraints'. For instance, an employer may provide limits for resources and time allocation with clients.

We do not solve problems in a vacuum. Apart from the 'rules' mentioned above, various factors determine the parameters of our thinking. In part, we are guided by our own *experience*. If you were asked to assist an individual who has difficulty eating you would need to know the cause of the difficulty: is it due to an intention tremor; spasticity; poor postural stability; a visual defect; stiff and painful joints? What is the exact difficulty? Does the spoon slip out of his/her grasp; is the distance between mouth and plate too great; does food fall off the spoon? Whether you choose to treat the underlying deficit or take a compensatory approach may depend on your knowledge and previous experience of this situation. However, another major factor that will determine your approach is the *context*. Are you, for instance, working with someone in their own home? Is the individual undertaking a rehabilitation programme? Is it a long-term problem? What are your employer's priorities? To what extent can family be relied on to help out? An experienced therapist uses both previous encounters with similar situations and understanding of environmental demands to guide problem solving.

To highlight a range of issues in problem solving, a story follows where the occupational therapist and her client are the key players. The scene is set in the client's home. The story begins with background information about the therapist and the scenario then considers a case that is typical of her daily work.

THE CONTEXT

The occupational therapist, Jenny, has a community-based job that involves working in their own homes with people who have physical disabilities. Typically, she uses compensatory techniques to deal with problems encountered within the home environment. It is important to understand the framework in which problem solving takes place, as this suggests the options available and the limitations of the problem-solving process. How is the framework defined? An important aspect of this initial phase where the problem is defined is the ability of the solver to limit the number of solutions considered. It would be unrealistic to consider endless possibilities every time a problem was identified – rather like looking for a needle in a haystack. Jenny knows where to look in the 'haystack' and so continues her search. The boundaries Jenny sets frame the problem and decisions are then made within this framework. The employer's expectation sets the scene for what should be dealt with and in this particular work setting, environmental modifications and teaching compensatory techniques are basic to the contribution made by the occupational therapist. The client also expects the occupational therapy service to provide assistance with tasks such as gaining access into their home, bathing and meal preparation. Thus social expectations will play a large part in defining Jenny's role and be a significant part of the environmental factors.

In addition, Jenny will bring her own expectations into the problem-solving process. These professional prejudices will be taken into every home she visits and have an impact on her course of action with each client. They will be shaped by influences such as previous encounters with clients, her negotiations with employers/funders and dialogue with other professionals. Before visiting this lady, Jenny would have a mindset about the kind of problem she was expecting. This would be affected by the information that was known such as the medical diagnosis, the person's age, their living situation and the reason for the referral as well as her expectations of the kind of problem that it is her business, as an occupational therapist, to deal with. So the professional judgements Jenny makes are a result of a complex blend of objective facts, other people's expectations and personal understandings of the situation.

Prejudices can be a real problem if they result in Jenny making up her mind before seeing the situation for herself or if they prevent her from listening to her client; for example, they may limit the type of solutions that are considered in a new situation. Luchins (1942) refers to this phenomenon as a *problem-solving set*.

Experience, then, is a two-edged sword – it can assist and give direction in solving problems but can also result in habits which limit our ability to consider alternative approaches.

Jenny has worked in this area for two years and has had extensive experience in the area of physical disability over an 18-year period prior to this. The last two years have enabled Jenny to develop expertise in the area of resources useful to modify the environment of people living in their own homes. She has, for instance, learned about the supply of small aids and equipment such as bath boards, rails and jar openers and, where necessary, how to supply and fit these. Also, she has developed expertise in the matter of major home alterations, what is available and how to process these through the system. Seating and wheelchair prescription are also demanding aspects of her current job. Her specific knowledge of disability and the implications for this on both present and future function is also helpful. For instance, knowing that a client was on the list to have a total hip replacement operation may influence the extent of the bathroom alterations recommended and would also require an understanding of how to fit out the environment to take account of postoperative precautionary measures.

Problem solving is dependent not just on the amount of knowledge brought to the situation but also its direct relationship to the context, i.e. an expert problem solver in the area of paediatrics will not usually be an expert problem solver in the area of geriatrics. Experience (i.e. frequent exposure to similar situations) allows the clinician to develop an organised, interrelated knowledge structure in long-term memory that makes knowledge easy to access.

Another important skill that Jenny has developed over time is the knack of asking questions that will identify functional difficulties. Listening to the client and responding to cues are really important to elicit the 'real' problem. Observation of function is also essential to determine not only what clients do but how they do it: are they safe, is *their* version of their ability the same as *your* interpretation of their performance? On a home visit there is not a great deal of time to come to grips with these issues and determine the solutions so it is important to be able to ask appropriate questions and make pertinent observations quickly. Finally, communication skills are also important to ensure that Jenny is able to convey the various options available so that the individual feels informed and able to participate in the problem-solving process.

A critical factor in problem solving is the knowledge base of the problem solver. Jenny keeps up to date with new developments and has attended study days, workshops and conferences to extend her knowledge. Reading journals and suppliers' catalogues also provides information about new equipment and techniques. Technology can bring about rapid change in the field of equipment so there is a need for ongoing education to keep abreast of current developments. Changes in the health field can also bring about modifications in the way that funding is distributed and health-care priorities established. Keeping up to date with current health policies is therefore essential when acting as a client advocate. For instance, in the situation being discussed, the community health services in New Zealand are currently being reviewed with the intention of devolving this to the private sector, a move that would have enormous consequences for the provision of an occupational therapy service.

THE SCENARIO

Jenny had been asked to visit an elderly lady, Mabel James, who had reported difficulty in bathing and getting out of the back door to hang up the laundry. The referral in this instance had come from her daughter who had given the reason for the problems as being 'arthritis in the hips'. One week after the referral, Jenny had organised to visit Mabel and was now driving to the given address contemplating the referral. Not an unusual scenario and on the surface it all seemed simple enough. In this situation Jenny will be able to call on knowledge gained in similar previous encounters to help her make sense of the present situation. This process is called *pattern matching* where experts access well-organised networks of knowledge in long-term memory. Novices do not have this type of memory to call on so they will use more analytical methods of problem solving which rely on developing a range of possible solutions and hypothesis generation. This is a slower process but is also used by experts in situations that are complex with unique characteristics.

Jenny's experience of this type of problem had enabled her to be reasonably certain of the outcome; of course, there could be all sorts of extraneous circumstances that could influence the outcome. Jenny remembered visiting an elderly man who had similar problems. When she arrived at his home and observed his mobility, she noticed with alarm that his hip seemed to be on the point of collapse. The indications were the excruciating pain he suffered when weight bearing, even when using a walking frame, an obvious limp to the left side and his extremely slow walking pace – he struggled even to get from room to room. This man had osteoarthritis in both hips, his spine and knees. Jenny contacted the doctor immediately for a review. The seriousness of the situation resulted in him having a total hip replacement operation within a few days. In this case, he had deteriorated very quickly from the time of referral. He was beyond occupational therapy assistance and required immediate operative intervention. Experience allowed Jenny to respond to salient information and change the course of enquiry as the clinical 'picture' evolved. In this instance, Jenny reframed the problem as being one for an orthopaedic surgeon.

Another unexpected situation occurred when Jenny visited a woman for similar reasons. Her husband had died three months earlier and he had been her main support person. He had hung out the washing, assisted with the shopping, paid the bills, driven the car and even helped her to get dressed. Without this support she was not coping at all well and was despairing of managing daily tasks again. This lady was still grieving following her loss and meanwhile no-one had ever noticed her difficulties.

The introduction of new factors into the equation can quickly change the 'known' into a serious challenge, like the client's unexpected grief response. In the course of occupational therapy practice, how does the serious challenge become the 'known'? How often would Jenny have to deal with a particularly challenging situation for it to become 'easy' the next time? These questions are difficult to answer, but we do know that expertise is characterised by frequent experience of similar situations. There is the potential here for more than one hypothesis: for example, Jenny may have postulated that difficulty with Activities of Daily Living (ADL) tasks had resulted from:

1 restriction of hip movement and pain;
2 lack of usual support;
3 grief reaction to husband's death.

Each of these scenarios would have different solutions. From Jenny's perspective the first could be dealt with by employing aids and equipment, the second by organising some assistance in the home. If neither of these resolved the issues, then the most realistic action may be to refer the client back to the GP so that her situation could be reviewed again, taking into account the new information with a possible recommendation that she be referred to a grief counsellor. Of course, all three actions could be taken simultaneously. This scenario illustrates restrictions that the occupational therapist should consider; in this particular job, the occupational therapist's role does not include that of a 'grief counsellor'.

To get back to Mabel's referral: in Jenny's experience difficulty getting out of the bath due to painful hips could also mean that the person had trouble getting out of chairs, on/off the toilet and in/out of bed. Rogers (1982) reported that within acute physical settings, the medical diagnosis was significant when occupational therapists developed a definition of the problem. Jenny illustrates this by beginning with the arthritis in the hip as the underlying factor. For instance, when you watch someone struggle to get off a chair you know that they would be unable to get off the toilet or off the bed easily. Furthermore, when hips and/or knees are involved you would suspect there might be problems reaching to the floor, so aids such as a toe drier, sock gutter or long shoehorn could be useful. Fatigue is another related problem, especially when the individual experiences pain when mobilising. Jenny has learned that signs of exertion when walking from one room to another could indicate problems with other tasks that require standing/walking for a period of time such as meal preparation and making a bed. Experience has taught Jenny to group together functional tasks that require similar physical abilities and to check for all of these if the individual identifies a problem with one task.

> Clustering related information together is a method used by experts to organise knowledge for easy recall so when they look at an apparently complicated situation they are able to represent it in terms of a small number of patterns or chunks. For example, in this instance the information is related to bio-mechanical features of tasks such as the amount of stress put through Mabel's hips when getting up from a seated position or when reaching forward to the floor.

DEFINING THE SITUATION

Jenny parked her car on the street a good distance from the flat as parking was at a premium in this area of town. As she walked up the path admiring the neatly kept rose garden she couldn't help wondering if Mabel could manage to weed and prune it without assistance.

A distraction in the form of a mangy grey cat appeared from the hedge and greeted her warmly. There was one six-inch step up to the porch then a further two-inch step up to the front door with a grab rail on the door frame. A knock resulted in a voice calling out 'Wait a minute'. Mabel opened the door a few moments later apologising for her slowness in walking as she used elbow crutches. Almost automatically, Jenny looked for cues. Something in the set-up of the environment or the way the person was walking, sitting or communicating may remind her of a situation she had previously encountered. This helped to create a mental image and triggered the generation of possible solutions – these provided a structure for interpreting the problem. Without the experience base, the novice does not form this mental picture.

Mabel greeted Jenny by name (no memory difficulties here) and asked her to step into the living room and take a seat; the cat at this point took advantage of the open door and rushed into the kitchen. A flighty cat – a possible hazard for Mabel? Could she reach to the floor to feed the cat? The flat was compact and in a housing complex for elderly people which was supported by the local council.

Jenny noticed that Mabel was competent with elbow crutches, i.e. she walked at a steady pace, balance was good and when sitting she was conscientious about placing the crutches safely on a small table to the left of her armchair. Everything was on this table! The surface was covered with the phone, the notebook with the phone numbers written out, glasses, newspaper, keys, purse and the *New Zealand Woman's Weekly*. Given her difficulties in mobility, this strategy of having all frequently used items in one place seemed very sensible. The armchair was high and firm. When asked about this, Mabel said that her family had bought it for her because she had problems getting out of her old one which had been lower and softer.

The ensuing discussion explored a range of daily living tasks and the history of the problem. Other than the identified problems, Jenny enquired in particular about her ability to get out of her armchair and to get off her bed. Mabel insisted that neither tasks was 'too' difficult for her although both took time and effort. However, she did report that getting up from the toilet was a problem. To check out other possibilities, Jenny asked about reaching down to her feet to do various self-care tasks but these were all within Mabel's capabilities and not causing her any concern. Finally, her ability to manage household tasks such as cooking and cleaning was investigated. There were no apparent issues for concern as Mabel had three daughters living locally who were very helpful; for example, they would have her around

---

Before meeting the client, the skilled problem solver will have a set of probing questions organised so that the situation can be defined and surrounding issues understood. For the bathing difficulty, examples of questions (modified from Wales, Nardi and Stager, 1993) would be:

Actors: Who was involved in the situation: family, spouse, neighbours, friends? Who reported the situation: client, doctor, family member?

Action: What happened when the client was bathing: was the client experiencing pain when weight bearing, slipping on the bottom of the bath? Could she reach the taps, judge the water temperature?

Environment: What type of bath was involved: plastic; iron? Was it a full-size bath, a 'scrub'? Was there a shower available and was this ever used? Was the shower over the bath; in a separate unit? Did it have a hand-held hose; was there a lip into the shower unit? Was there a bath mat, a rail?

Scene: When does the client have difficulty: stepping into the bath, getting out? Is this on all occasions or only when the weather affects her arthritis?

Cause: Why does she experience difficulty: is there pain, restriction of movement in the joints? Does she have a respiratory problem; a heart condition? Memory loss; anxiety?

Consequences: How serious is the issue: has she hurt herself; has she fallen? Does she never take a bath unless someone is there to help her? Is her level of hygiene acceptable?

Responses to these questions add further knowledge to the therapist's mental image of the situation.

---

to their homes for a meal at the weekend and give her frozen meals to take back to her flat. The daughters also helped with tasks such as vacuuming and cleaning the bath but Mabel was capable of doing all regular household tasks so long as she took her time. Neighbours also assisted with tasks such as bringing in the laundry or collecting the mail.

The interview confirmed the referral information that Mabel's concerns were bathing and getting out of her back door to hang up the laundry, but it also identified one other issue related to toileting. Once a working diagnosis is made, solutions may be trialled. Solutions may not always give rise to a satisfactory outcome, in which case the information needs to be analysed again with the new data from the 'failed' solutions added.

Satisfied that the problems had been identified, Jenny asked Mabel to go to the bathroom with her to describe the difficulties in this area. The bath was normal height and had a hand shower over it. Mabel gave a detailed account of the contortions she had to go through to get out of the bath and indicated that she was afraid of falling. Jenny discussed the simple solution of a bath board or a bath seat and a rail to support her when getting in and out of the bath. Mabel was most impressed with these possibilities but she also expressed some reluctance about substituting a shower for the bath – she did enjoy a good soak. There was a rail attached to the wall near the toilet and Mabel demonstrated that the problem was that the rail was too far forward and resulted in her putting a great deal of weight through her hip before being able to use the rail effectively. Jenny decided that there were two likely solutions for this problem: one was to reposition the rail and install a raised toilet seat; the other was to provide a raised toilet frame. Jenny suggested a raised toilet frame rather than the toilet seat and rail as Mabel needed the stability that this would provide.

The pair then proceeded to the back door to consider easier access to the washing line. There was one two-inch step down to the porch then two steps down to the path that led to the clothes line. Mabel currently managed to carry items to the line by using only one crutch and carrying items of clothing over her arm or in a small basket. The pegs were carried in a cotton bag slung around her neck. Mabel indicated that the process of weight bearing on one leg at a time as she descended the steps caused her considerable pain. Her neighbours assisted with large items such as the sheets. Jenny suggested that a solid rail should be put down one side of the steps to the path and a grab rail placed on the frame of the door.

While there may be a range of solutions, the funders will usually only finance the minimum needed to achieve independence. However, on occasion the occupational therapist may want to make a case to the funder for more than what may seem 'reasonable'. For instance, if a ramp were requested in this instance, a special case would have to be made using a logical, valid argument based on problem-solving principles.

TAKING ACTION AND EVALUATING THE RESULTS

Jenny had some of the necessary equipment with her so went to the car and assembled this while Mabel sat down for a rest. Once Jenny returned carrying the relevant aids and the bag with the drill and handrails, they both went to the bathroom. The bath seat was trialled first; assistance was still needed for Mabel to get out of the bath so the bath board was then tried. This was heralded as a great success so Jenny showed her how to fit it securely then found the stud in the wall and attached a small vertical grab rail.

Mabel practised using the equipment by having a 'dry run' shower under Jenny's watchful eye and was delighted. To ensure that instructions had been fully understood, the process was repeated.

Jenny thought how straightforward this was and could remember another occasion when the lady in question had similar difficulties and high expectations that a rail would solve all her problems. When she discovered that more assistance would be needed she was adamant that she wanted to get into the bath for a soak and insisted that indeed she would do this. No amount of rational explanation about how her current struggles caused tremendous tension would deter her from the memory of a blissful soak in the bath. Jenny had to leave her with the rail and trust that she would change her mind at a later date. She did, but it took an incident which left her trapped in the bath for several hours to finally convince her that a wet area shower was the only safe solution. Later, she sheepishly admitted to Jenny that she really enjoyed her shower.

Jenny's solution doesn't necessarily meet the needs of the individual as they may have other priorities. Constraints to solutions are not only presented by the employer but also by the client themselves who may determine limits.

Such situations raise ethical dilemmas in problem-solving.

- There is the notion that identifying a problem that you (as an occupational therapist) can deal with makes you useful and keeps you in a job. You could leave a bath seat knowing that, if it were used, the client would be safer.
- A problem may be identified which you feel should be addressed but the client does not want you to deal with it. Should you have even pursued the information about the problem in the first place? For instance, during a home visit to an elderly woman you notice she has bruising on her face which you enquire about. It transpires that her son has been abusing her but she is adamant that she does not want you to do anything about it.
- Finally, a problem is identified which you feel should be addressed but it is not in the remit of your particular job, e.g. to be 'grief counsellor' as described in an earlier scenario.

Having been satisfied that there were no further issues and that Mabel was happy with her level of independence and safe with all daily tasks, Jenny informed Mabel that a contractor would be around to fit the outdoor rails and James the storeman would drop off the toilet frame. Jenny picked up her tools and the unused bath seat and returned to the car. As anticipated in the beginning, this was a straightforward case where a bath board, rail and a raised toilet frame in the bathroom and rails at the back door solved Mabel's current problems. All that remained to do was to relay information to those who would issue the outstanding equipment, then record the problems and the action taken. Once all modifications had been made, a phone call to Mabel to ensure that everything was satisfactory would be the final evaluation.

> In occupational therapy, as in medicine, the general nature of the goal is known before the situation is defined. Thus the general goal of independence and safety in the home environment would translate to more specific goals after the initial data collection; in this scenario the specific goals relate to independence in bathing, toileting and managing the laundry safely.

DISCUSSION

Solving problems involves developing an understanding of the problem (i.e. defining it) and the subsequent solving process. It can be seen from this scenario that Jenny spent a relatively large proportion of her time with Mabel *defining the problem*. This involves first of all understanding the situation you are in. Jenny must be able to consider the particular circumstances of the client; this means understanding her level of disability and discomfort, her social situation, motivation and environmental barriers imposed by the home. Second, the goal(s) must be understood; the client's goals may be different from those of the therapist. There was apparent agreement between Mabel and Jenny that independence in bathing, toileting and managing the laundry were the important issues. Once Jenny was well orientated to the problems, solutions were proposed; this is the *solving process* which took much less time than the initial defining process.

During a home visit, both the assessment of the situation and the solutions must be determined in a relatively short period of time. An experienced therapist will depend on domain-specific knowledge acquired through past experience to collect, interpret information and devise ideas for action. The environment, both Mabel's home situation and the employer's expectations, will set the scene for decision making and provide limits to the solutions considered. Last, but not least, the client will also be a major factor in the determination of a reasonable solution; there is no point in devising a solution that apparently will be the 'best' for the client when in fact the client is unlikely to follow your suggestions or heed your advice. Therapists often need to find creative ways of meeting clients' needs and ensuring safety and maximum independence for all concerned.

It is important to note that problem solving is a logical process. Intelligent action is based on well-thought out plans which are a response to an identified problem. Each of the decisions in this process depends on those preceding it. The importance of the initial data collection/analysis can be illustrated by returning to the problem outlined at the beginning of this chapter, where our neighbour was concerned about her waterlogged property. The problem was originally defined by a drainage engineer who assessed the situation and came up with the following decisions:

Problem: An old drain had cracked.
Plan: Locate the drain and replace it.
Action: Dig and find the drain (this work was carried out by a plumber).
Evaluation: There was no sign of a drain anywhere near the spot identified by the engineer. Review the problem!

This new information resulted in the plumber doing his own investigation. Conclusion? The seepage came from the sump, not from the pipe. The drainage engineer reviewed his stance on where the drain was located – no, it didn't do a 90° turn as had previously been indicated! The pipe went straight ahead and couldn't possibly be the cause of the problem.

Revised problem: The sump was leaking around the insertion of the drainpipe.
Plan: Fill the gap.
Action: Concrete was mixed and applied to the faulty sump.
Evaluation: No water seepage in the neighbour's garden. Success!

This drainpipe saga illustrates that the analysis of information at the outset is crucial. In the case of the drain, all relevant information was to hand but it was wrongly interpreted. One faulty assumption or preconceived idea about the situation can lead to incorrect interpretation of the facts. Alternatively, when our feelings are aroused we may act first and think later without taking a more objective, critical approach to the situation. Defining the problem accurately requires intelligent use of appropriate knowledge and experience and an exploration of all relevant avenues. Effective problem solving is based on evidence that arises from the available cues and data; it is a thinking process that is both creative, as hypotheses are developed, and critical, as solutions are evaluated.

At the end of the day, successful decision makers must be able to bring order from confusion. In occupational therapy, as described in this chapter, rational problem-solving processes will ensure the best possible outcomes for our clients.

Further thoughts

1 This chapter highlights the importance of making choices and choosing the hypothesis which best fits. Taking a specific problem, highlight two or more hypotheses and map out the different routes and their consequences.
2 Think of a client's problem which you have recently solved. Focus on the key decisions you made and reflect on these. Would you do it the same way again?
3 Cues and pattern recognition are significant for effective decision making. In your area of practice, articulate the cues which you routinely look for to build your patterns. Share this with another.

REFERENCES

Luchins, A. S. (1942) Mechanisation in problem solving. *Psychological Monographs*, 54(6), Whole No. 248.

Rogers, J. C. (1982) Reasoning of occupational therapists during the initial assessment of physically disabled patients. *Occupational Therapy Journal of Research*, 2(4), 195–219.

Wales, C. E., Nardi, A. H., Stager, R. (1993) Emphasising critical thinking and problem solving. In L. Curry and J. F. Wergin and Associates, (eds) *Educating Professionals*. Jossey-Bass, San Francisco.

FURTHER READING

Benner, P. (1984) *From Novice to Expert: Excellence and Power in Clinical Nursing Practice*. Addison-Wesley, Reading, MA.

Chi, M. T. H., Glaser, R. (1985) Problem solving ability. In R. J. Sternberg (ed.) *Human Abilities. An Information Processing Approach*. W. H. Freeman, New York.

Elstein, A. S., Schulman, L. S., Sprafka, S. A. (1978) *Medical Problem Solving: An Analysis of Clinical Reasoning*. Harvard University Press, Cambridge, MA.

Fleming, M. (1994) Procedural reasoning: addressing functional limitations. In C. Mattingly and M. Fleming (eds), *Clinical Reasoning: Forms of Inquiry in a Therapeutic Practice*. F. A. Davis, Philadelphia.

Higgs, J., Jones, M. (eds) (1995) *Clinical Reasoning in the Health Professions*. Butterworth-Heinemann, Oxford. (See Section Two where authors examine clinical reasoning in medicine, nursing, physiotherapy and occupational therapy. Problem-solving principles are explained in relation to each of the disciplines).

Kassirer, J. P., Kopelman, R. I. (1991) *Learning Clinical Reasoning*. Williams & Wilkins, Baltimore.

Robertson, L. J. (1996) Clinical reasoning, part 1. The nature of problem solving: a literature review. *British Journal of Occupational Therapy*, 59(4), 178–182.

Robertson, L. J. (1996) Clinical reasoning, part 2. Novice/expert differences. *British Journal of Occupational Therapy*, 59(5), 212–216.

Rogers, J. C. (1983) Eleanor Clarke Slagle Lectureship 1983. Clinical reasoning: the ethics, science and art. *American Journal of Occupational Therapy*, 37(9), 601–616.

Schon, D. (1983) *The Reflective Practitioner*. Basic Books, New York. (See Chapter Two in particular, 'From Technical Rationality to Reflection in Action', which discusses the complexity of converting an uncertain situation into a problem that can be solved.)

Tamm, M. (1996) Ethical dilemmas encountered by community-based occupational therapists in home care setting. *Scandinavian Journal of Occupational Therapy*, 3, 180–187.

Voss, J. F., Tyler, W. T., Yengo, L. A. (1983) Individual differences in the solving of social science problems. In R. F. Dillon and R. R. Schmeck (eds), *Individual Differences in Cognition, Vol. 1*. Academic Press, New York.

3 WORKING OUT: WORKING WITH ANGELICA – INTERPRETING PRACTICE

Chris Chapparo

KEY POINTS
- Acute neurorehabilitation; head injury
- Theory of planned behaviour
- Personal reasoning
- Multidimensional inductive–hypothetical–deductive reasoning

In Angelica's story the two therapists' reasoning is set within the theory of planned behaviour which is an innovative way of analysing thinking. The author proposes that each therapist views practice through a personal reality which impacts on all therapeutic behaviour. This personal reality includes ethical issues; for example, the age of the person and the intensity of interventions. It also challenges the three-track linear model of clinical reasoning. The potential use of video recording as a tool for reflecting on practice is also considered.

CASE STUDY   Angelica's story

Diane and Michelle are occupational therapists, master clinicians, who have worked for five years with people who have had traumatic brain injury. It is 10 am; they wheel Angelica into the occupational therapy treatment area in a reclining wheelchair. Angelica is 18, blonde, pretty and thin, and is an inpatient on the neuro ward of a large hospital. She was a passenger in a car accident that left her comatosed for some weeks. She wears a track suit. Her head falls to one side; her legs are stiffly extended; her arms and wrists are held in rigid flexion; a urinal bag is attached to the side of her chair. She has freshly painted pink nails, that peep out from the hand splints she wears on both hands. Above the locket she wears around her neck, there is evidence of a newly closed tracheotomy. She maintains a fixed stare, unresponsive to anyone or anything around her. Closely following Angelica is her mother, who comes to most therapy sessions, and who has just helped Diane dress Angelica. After kissing her daughter on the forehead, she sits off to one side and watches intently, offering little comment throughout the therapy session.

For the next half hour, Michelle and Diane work in concert to transfer Angelica onto a raised mat. In unspoken agreement, they assume specific positions to control Angelica's body as they teach her to roll and come to sitting, just as she would if she were getting out of bed. In sitting, they again work as a team to obtain some more consistent affective responses from Angelica as they attempt to get her to look at pictures of herself, her home and her friends, at objects that she uses every day; to look at her mother. Michelle supports Angelica from behind and becomes her external support system. Diane sits in front, directing Angelica's actions, questioning, admonishing, joking, praising, reinforcing, physically guiding, talking with Angelica and her mother without missing a beat. Diane tries to get Angelica to use an electronic switch mechanism to indicate a consistent 'yes' or 'no' response. To the observer, Angelica remains unresponsive. At the end of the session, Diane and Michelle transfer Angelica back into her chair and make some mechanical adjustments. Her mother lovingly straightens Angelica's clothes, redoes her hair and puts on her hand splints, while Diane talks with her about what she saw, why she did what she did in therapy and what her mother could do with Angelica before tomorrow's session.

THE INTERPRETATION

This therapy session contains many elements that characterise the person–environment–activity focus of occupational therapy intervention for people who have sustained severe traumatic brain injury (Christiansen and Baum, 1997; Ylvisaker, 1985). First, intervention targets the multiple physical, cognitive, sensory and psychosocial aspects of Angelica's occupational performance (Chapparo and Ranka, 1995; Dutton, 1995). Second, intervention is individually structured to suit Angelica's specific needs. Third, Angelica's physical, sociocultural and sensory environment is factored into the goals and procedures used by the therapists. Fourth, the focus is on Angelica's active engagement in everyday occupations. The session 'fits' a textbook description of what constitutes occupational therapy management of someone like Angelica (Kovich and Bermann, 1988). Using this knowledge, as well as the multiple cues evident throughout the session, the skilled observer could develop a procedural explanation of the clinical reasoning processes used by Diane and Michelle that resulted in this therapy session (see, for example, Bridge and Twible, 1997; Dutton, 1995; Fleming, 1994; Higgs and Jones, 1995). However, this explanation would not fully explain why these therapists treated Angelica in the particular way they did. It was clear that the session was not just a series of actions resulting from a cognitively structured line of thought, but a purposeful social interaction among four people that was intensely and personally relevant to all participants. With this in mind, several further questions arise from the observation of the session.

What did the therapists think about as they treated Angelica? What personal factors impacted on their decisions? Did the context of treatment influence what they decided to do? What attitudes did they hold about their own ability to treat Angelica and did those attitudes influence their actions? What beliefs did they hold about the treatment and did those beliefs determine what treatment looked like? Did they do what they intended to do? How did they prioritise and focus their actions in that particular way? How did they sustain their enthusiasm and thinking in order to treat Angelica day after day with seemingly little return? Was Angelica the central focus of clinical reasoning?

This chapter employs attitude–behaviour theory, specifically the theory of planned behaviour (Azjen, 1985; Azjen and Madden, 1986) to answer some of these questions and to explain how the therapists organised their thinking into a process of decision making that directed therapy. Narratives from the therapists' perceptions of the session are used to illustrate specific examples of therapist thinking.

THE THEORY OF PLANNED BEHAVIOUR

The theory of planned behaviour (Azjen, 1985; Ajzen and Madden, 1986) is based on the assumption that humans are reasoning beings who, in deciding what action to take in any given purposeful social situation, systematically process and utilise all the information available to them. It is a theory that deals with the relations among four major constructs: beliefs, attitudes, intentions and behaviour. These constructs, as presented in the theory of planned behaviour, are fundamentally motivational in nature. In relation to clinical reasoning in occupational therapy, the theory refers to what therapists choose to do in therapy as *intention* and asserts that intention to perform a particular activity in therapy is the immediate antecedent of any therapist's behaviour. The theory specifies three conceptually independent determinants of intention. One is a personal factor termed *attitude toward the behaviour* and refers to the degree to which therapists have a favourable or unfavourable evaluation of their own actions. The second predictor of intention is the *subjective norm*. This is a social factor which refers to the perceived social pressure to perform or not to perform specific therapy acts. The third determinant of intention, *perceived behavioural control*, refers to the therapist's belief as to how easy or difficult it will be to carry out intended therapy (Ajzen and Madden, 1986; Chapparo, 1997). As demonstrated by Chapparo (1997), a fourth determinant of intention is found when studying clinical reasoning of occupational therapists. This has been termed the *personal norm* and can be thought of as pretheoretical positions therapists hold about the nature of humans and life. Under different therapy circumstances, attitudes, subjective norms, perceived behavioural control or personal norms will predominantly influence intention and therefore therapist decision making.

The theory of planned behaviour also deals with the antecedents of these determinants of intention, antecedents which in the final analysis determine therapist intentions and therapy actions. As interpreted by Chapparo (1997), the theory proposes that therapy is a function of salient information or beliefs relevant to the specific therapy situation. Four kinds of beliefs have been identified as influencing clinical reasoning: *behavioural beliefs* (what therapists believe will be the outcome of therapy), *normative beliefs* (what therapists believe other relevant people think

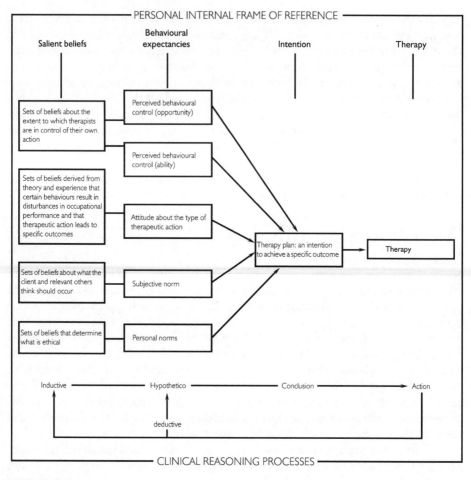

Figure 3.1

The clinical reasoning process using concepts from the theory of planned behaviour.

they should do in therapy), *control beliefs* (beliefs about the presence or absence of resources and skills with which to carry out therapy) and *personal beliefs* (what therapists believe should happen in therapy, based on personal notions of humanity and quality of life). The relationship between all these constructs is illustrated in Figure 3.1 and is termed the therapist's *internal frame of reference* (Chapparo, 1997). In this chapter, Diane's and Michelle's narratives are used to explain how each of these constructs can be linked to form a line of reasoning that results in specific therapy action.

SUBJECTIVE NORMS AND CLINICAL REASONING

The theory of planned behaviour identifies the subjective norm as a social predictor of intended behaviour. In the thinking of these two therapists, it refers to the social pressure to engage in specific forms of therapy. In the treatment described, this social pressure was derived from two main sources: therapist perceptions of what Angelica and her mother wanted and expected from therapy, and therapist perceptions of what other professional members of the team expected them to do.

Subjective norms were formed partly by the therapists' perceptions about Angelica's discharge environment; perceptions of Angelica's abilities and disabilities as well as her mother's ability to care for her; perceptions of the extent to which Angelica and her mother had insight into existing problems; perceptions of the relationships between Angelica, her mother and the therapists; and visions of Angelica's future potential. These perceptions can be viewed as a store of knowledge that contributes to the internal reality of the therapist and are expressed as internal beliefs. From internal beliefs, a motivation to comply with the expectations of others is generated. In turn, motivation prompts an intention to engage in a specific pattern of therapy (treatment plan). When this intention is carried out, occupational therapy (the behaviour) is viewed as 'meeting the needs' of the client or carer and/or 'fitting in' with expectations of other members of the team. It was evident throughout Diane's and Michelle's narratives that more than one of these expectations were considered at any one time in one treatment session. Only a limited sampling only is possible in this chapter.

The links between therapist perceptions of people's expectations (beliefs), the resulting subjective norms (behavioural expectancy), the intention to act in a particular way (treatment plan) and the actual therapy (behaviour) can be illustrated as shown in Figure 3.2.

In line with this model, the narratives of the two therapists demonstrate a causal line of thinking between their salient beliefs about what others think therapy should

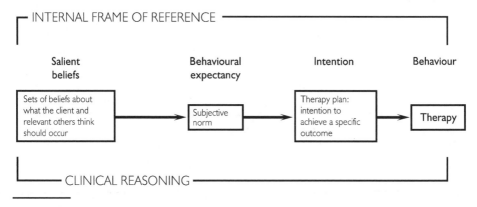

Figure 3.2

Beliefs, subjective norms, intention (therapy plan) and therapy.

be, their own expectations of therapy as a result of those beliefs and creation of an intended therapy plan that acts in accordance with those expectations. For example, in talking through her treatment, Diane states:

> *Her mother's expectations are high. She expects us to see Angelica several times a day for as long as it takes to get her to respond and come out of coma. I suppose it is her expectation that we be as patient and as dedicated as she is.*

Diane articulates a strongly held belief about the therapy expectations of Angelica's mother. Decisions that Diane makes about how often Angelica is seen and for how long are motivated by this belief. After a period of many weeks when Angelica finally goes home, Diane judges the outcome of treatment against this expectation.

> *I think her mother was disappointed in us – like – we weren't able to give her daughter back.*

Further into the narrative, Diane explains a particular hypothetico–deductive line of thinking that demonstrates how her subjective belief about what Angelica expected from therapy, led to her forming an image of the outcome of therapy. Intentions created by this belief resulted in a particular therapy activity that was in concert with what she believed were Angelica's expectations. This hypothetico–deductive reasoning style had three dimensions that could be termed '*given that*', '*then*' and '*therefore*'. '*Given that*' refers to the therapist's perception of the mother's or Angelica's expectations of therapy and is the starting point for decision making. '*Then*' refers to the predicted outcome of therapy relative to that expectation. '*Therefore*' refers to the intended therapy plan that is created. First, Diane created several possible client expectations of therapy (*given that*). This served to extend her own knowledge of what she perceived Angelica wanted from therapy. Then, she created several possible therapy scenarios that would meet these expectations (*then*). Finally, she described the conclusion – the final form of part of therapy (*therefore*).

> **Given that:** . . . *she expects to have a bit of fun . . . not just be constantly instructed. She expects me to tell her what to do in different ways. I think she expects me to help her choose. She probably expects therapy to be hard work . . .*
> **Then:** *it has to be something she enjoys more than just sitting in a chair being stretched . . . she has to have some choice . . . she has to gain some independence.*
> **Therefore:** *I get her out of her chair and we work on communicating, playing games, listening to her music. I'm sure she knows when she gets into that position and she says to herself 'Oooh yes . . .' she knows it's time for fun and hard work because it's something she enjoys more than sitting in that chair.*

Here, Diane generated three expectations that she perceived Angelica had of therapy (*given that*), including Angelica's personal expectation (fun), Angelica's expectation of Diane (type of instruction) and Angelica's expectation of the form of therapy (work: getting out of the chair). From this set of hypotheses the therapist created three further hypotheses (*then*) about what therapy should look like (something not sitting in a chair: choice and demonstrating independence). Finally, (*therefore*) Diane chose to work for part of the session sitting on the side of the plinth (not sitting in a chair); letting Angelica explore her own ability to indicate 'yes' or 'no' through a communication switch (choice and independence) and visualising ('Oooh yes . . .') Angelica's enjoyment (fun). Actual therapy matched Diane's intentions. Her intention matched the expected outcome for therapy that she created. This outcome was developed from sets of beliefs about what she perceived Angelica wanted.

The same hypothetico–deductive thinking process was used when considering another aspect of subjective norms: Angelica's abilities and disabilities. In Diane's narrative, it was evident that she created an 'internally constructed conversation' with Angelica, who was non-verbal, whereby Diane played the part of both Angelica and herself. Specifically, in this example, Diane describes 'how she knows' that Angelica's cognitive abilities are responding to therapy.

> *When she (Angelica) was sitting at the table . . . she knew what she was trying to do . . .*
>
> Given that: *she followed her hand to the switch. She knew where it was going. I could see she was trying to get her hand there. She was persevering. Normally she goes 'I can't do it . . . aaagh!' and gets upset. She was following her hand with her eyes.*
> Then: *she concentrated quite a long time, you know it was kind of 'aaagh' her noise, and she was prepared to be calmed down and keep going.*
> Therefore: *she understood cause and effect . . . so I kept going.*

Here Diane used information about what she believed Angelica's abilities were (subjective norm). These were developed through a number of hypotheses that were generated to explain Angelica's behaviour towards a communication switch mechanism. The resulting motivation or intention to continue (therapy plan) resulted in Diane continuing with this particular activity (therapy).

Diane's narrative contained more internally constructed dialogue with Angelica relative to her beliefs about the expected relationship between herself and Angelica. She converted Angelica's limited gestural and expression cues into a verbal response in her imagination. She then used this information either to determine what to do next in therapy or to confirm that her actions were in line with what she perceived were Angelica's expectations of the therapeutic relationship.

> Interviewer: *so Angelica expects you to keep her safe . . . At what point do you know she needs help?*
> Given that: *she'd show it in her face that she had had it. She might turn and look at me . . . and go (imitates Angelica's crying noise) and that's like saying 'No . . . I don't want to . . .'*
> Then: *so I'd clap my hands in front of her and say 'look' or 'show me' and pull a face and she'd go like this (demonstrates exaggerated blinking).*

Therefore: *then she'd sit there and make a good attempt at what I asked. I know I can keep going. She just needs to feel safe.*

The therapist describes what she believes is one of the paramount rules of the relationship between herself and Angelica: safety. Diane generates several hypotheses based on her knowledge that Angelica will tell her when she does not feel safe (*given that*). These lead to several hypothetical instructional solutions that are generated (*then*) to facilitate Angelica to continue with the task (*therefore*).

As outlined earlier, the therapists' decision making was influenced not only by the expectations of Angelica and her mother, but also by expectations of other professionals. In some instances, the perceptions of what other team members thought they as occupational therapists 'should do' became the central focus of reasoning. For example, Michelle says:

Given that: *the speech therapist is focused on what Angelica can respond to when she is asked something. So they see me in line with technology . . . they're almost at a bit of a loss as to what they can do with her . . .*
Then: *so they are probably looking to me as . . . well . . . what can we do with her . . . where do you put the switch . . . how can we help her reach it?*
Therefore: *so I work on the switch and then I show them things they can do with the switch . . .*

In part of this therapy session, Michelle's actions were aligned with the perceived expectation of the speech therapist.

THEORY AND THE CLINICAL REASONING PROCESS

Theory and knowledge of disease have been given a prominent place in clinical reasoning literature (Higgs and Jones, 1995; Mattingly and Fleming, 1994). Many studies have demonstrated a hypothetico–deductive reasoning process that is used by therapists when they apply science and theory to the selection of occupational therapy intervention (Fleming, 1994; Parham, 1987; Rogers, 1983, 1986; Schell and Cervero, 1993). However, narratives from this treatment session support the notion that practical and theoretical knowledge about therapy and its expected outcomes are expressed as sets of internally held therapist beliefs (Chapparo, 1997). These are derived from theory and experience that confirm the existence of certain disturbances in occupational performance and that therapeutic action will lead to specific and beneficial outcomes. Emanating from these and other sets of beliefs outlined in Figure 3.1, attitudes about the effectiveness and value of types of therapy are constructed. These attitudes impact on decisions made by therapists about what therapy is planned (*intention*) and how they carry it out (*therapy*). This particular line of reasoning can be illustrated as shown in Figure 3.3.

The following narrative illustrates an example of this reasoning process similar to 'procedural reasoning' described by Fleming (1994, p. 136). Michelle was rolling Angelica from side to side, stopping to rotate and stretch her trunk on either side.

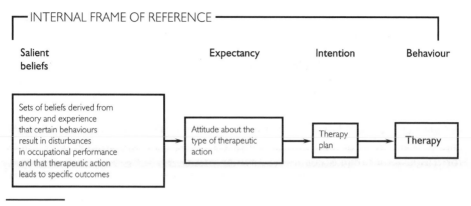

Figure 3.3

Theoretical and practical knowledge, attitudes and clinical reasoning.

The 'given that', 'then', 'therefore' pattern of thinking is again apparent, with an added '*because*' category that explains the theoretical foundation of the line of thought.

> Given that: *I want to teach her how to get out of bed.*
> Then: *she has to know how to roll.*
> Therefore: *I have to teach her the motor skills required to roll . . . I have to get the range she needs . . . I have to reduce her trunk rigidity . . . so I practise and practise and stretch her out to loosen her up.*
> Because: *the literature says that in the beginning stages of learning you have to break a task down into steps and practise before you can put it all together.*

Superficial examples of procedural reasoning were abundant in the therapists' narratives of this treatment session. Clear examples of procedural reasoning that were not fundamentally influenced by other team members, personal values or contextual factors were rare. In most instances, Diane and Michelle reasoned from the viewpoint of their own personally constructed theories, such as those termed 'reflection-in-action' by Schon (1987). In many instances where the therapists' theoretical knowledge was inadequate (*because*), they used the hypothetico–deductive mode of reasoning to experiment with the clinical situation by imagining multiple causes of the problem or outcomes to possible therapy scenarios. For example, in this part of Michelle's narrative, she questions why Angelica wasn't making expected gains from her handling.

> Given that: *I can't think of any reason why her shoulders should be so stiff.*
> Then: *I'm thinking . . . I haven't done this for a while and she has lost practice. I was wondering whether she has had any other neurological change. She wasn't rolling too well either. Maybe getting dressed this morning was stressful. I can't put it down to one thing.*

Therefore: *I'll let it go today . . . see how she does next time . . . I've seen this before with her. It won't do any good to worry her mother.*

Michelle constructed multiple hypotheses about the reason for the problem of increased stiffness in Angelica's shoulders through an internal reflective process that drew information from all theory and practical knowledge available to her. Her final action, to 'let it go for today', is based on a personal knowledge of Angelica and her mother, a personal decision that worrying Angelica's mother with more investigation would be of no use. This decision was the basis of her action and was made for reasons other than occupational therapy theory.

CONTROL BELIEFS: PERCEIVED BEHAVIOURAL CONTROL AND THE REASONING PROCESS

Perceived behavioural control refers to therapists' beliefs about how easy or difficult carrying out therapy is likely to be. In this session, control beliefs are derived from two sources. One related to therapists' perceptions about contextual elements of therapy, such as time, available resources and ethos of the treatment environment. The second related to perceptions of their own skilled ability to carry out the planned treatment. In Figures 3.1 and 3.4, these two sources are referred to as perceived behavioural control (*opportunity*) and perceived behavioural control (*ability*). These are similar to those reported by Schell and Cervero (1993) who described a facet of occupational therapy clinical reasoning as pragmatic reasoning which was further developed by Chapparo (1997).

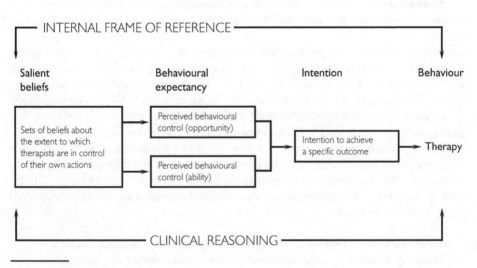

Figure 3.4

Control beliefs and clinical reasoning.

PERCEIVED BEHAVIOURAL CONTROL (OPPORTUNITY)

It has been demonstrated that time, resources and departmental ethos are contextual factors that influence therapist decision making (Chapparo, 1997). These same contextual factors impacted on therapist thinking in this session. The following part of Michelle's narrative demonstrates the same hypothetico–deductive reasoning process that links perceived behavioural control (opportunity) in terms of time to her proposed therapy plan.

> Interviewer: *what would make therapy more successful?*
> Given that: *time . . . heaps more time. At least another whole session. We've got so many things to work on . . . like seating . . .*
> Then: *I'm going to have to try a different recliner chair. I want to get a different headrest on. I'm going to have to figure out where to put her communication board. We're going to have to work on trunk supports and a pelvic strap . . .*
> Therefore: *but to do that is going to take a whole other session . . .*

She creates several hypotheses about what could be achieved if she had the opportunity (more time). Michelle describes a hypothetical course of thinking that is not related to diagnosis (as found in diagnostic reasoning) or a search for the link between the presenting problem and treatment selection. The problem requiring treatment is clearly stated the goal of the therapy is clearly stated, and the course of planned action is clearly stated. These are then 'put on hold' and are evaluated against the knowledge that the therapist has about the perceived opportunity (time) to carry out the planned treatment. Time was perceived as a contextual element that inhibited successful initiation of planned therapy. Although an alternative form of therapy was carried out (rolling), it was not judged by Michelle as fully effective. For example, when questioned about what she thought she had achieved in the session, Michelle states:

> *What do I feel I achieved? Not a huge amount other than the fact that I feel she can roll a bit better.*

CONTROL BELIEFS: PERCEIVED BEHAVIOURAL CONTROL (SKILL) AND THE REASONING PROCESS

As conceptualised in Figures 3.1 and 3.4, perceived behavioural control contains an element that is not contextually based, but derived from therapists' personal knowledge about their level of skill or ability to carry out the therapy they think is required. As Michelle watched a videotape of herself trying to get Angelica to sit independently over the edge of the mat, she expressed her frustration with that particular aspect of the session.

> Interviewer: *Did you get frustrated with that?*
> Michelle: *yes!*

As her narrative proceeded, Michelle then revealed a process of reasoning whereby she generated multiple hypotheses about why her treatment methods weren't successful for sitting.

> Given that: . . . *when you're teaching someone something and it's blatantly obvious to you that it's not getting across . . .*
> Then: *I was thinking – constantly reviewing in my mind what she was doing and thinking whether I should continue with this tack or go off onto another method. How far am I going to get? Why wouldn't she stay up today? Was it the way I was handling her?*
> Therefore: *I tried another way . . . but that just confused her more.*

Although Michelle actually carried out the planned treatment, her perception was that the session was not successful, based on her lack of skill in stimulating better sitting. She sums up her lack of control relative to skill as follows:

> *In this session I really wish I was an NDT therapist. There are ways to get better sitting . . . not knowing them is a disadvantage. I just couldn't work out how to get through to her.*

These aspects of the therapists' narratives indicate that what they remembered most vividly was not what was actually achieved, but the following relative to their own actions:

- failure to operationalise what was considered the best therapy plan;
- failure to achieve an ideal therapy goal;
- feelings of lack of control due to inadequate time and skill.

Positive and negative aspects of therapy are remembered relative to how easy or difficult it was to achieve an intended goal. It is likely that 'remembered' specific therapy experiences will further contribute to the therapists' internal control beliefs and personal knowledge stores about what is achievable within their particular contexts and ability and will influence future decision making.

PERSONAL NORMS AND THE CLINICAL REASONING PROCESS

Polanyi (1966, p. 52) suggested that all knowledge has a personal element or an inner set of assumptions, which he refers to as a 'framework of commitment'. Treatment decisions derived for this one session with Angelica were heavily influenced by the therapists' personal beliefs on two levels. First, personal beliefs about the nature of humans and associated quality of life were intimately involved with their personal expectations of therapy outcomes and hence, its relative success or failure – despite the expectations from other elements discussed. Second, personal beliefs related to faith and hope for the future and were linked to the extent to which individual therapists were willing to persevere with treating Angelica, a person with severe disability.

Weighting of personal values and beliefs to achieve an outcome that is personally acceptable to the therapist is a process of reasoning most obviously seen in situations of ethical dilemma. However, this type of reasoning was not only confined to situations of ethical dilemma in the session described in this chapter. Threads of a personally driven form of reasoning, based on salient personal beliefs, were routinely found in the multiple decisions made about actions throughout the session. This aspect of reasoning will therefore be termed 'personal reasoning' in this chapter. The personal beliefs held by the two therapists were individual and numerous. The process of personal reasoning followed a similar 'given that', 'then' and 'therefore' process to that outlined for other areas of knowledge use described previously. In this instance, 'given that' refers to statements about the personal beliefs held by the therapist relative to Angelica's specific situation. 'Then' refers to various alternative courses of action that the therapists can take or are directed to take by others and the reconciliation of them with the stated belief. 'Therefore' is the final action decided on by the therapist after reconciliation of a personal position on Angelica's situation.

THE NATURE OF HUMANS, QUALITY OF LIFE AND CLINICAL REASONING PROCESS

When talking about Angelica, Michelle states:

> Given that: *Angelica has her whole life ahead of her, she's deserving of input. I think she deserves the very best chance. Through no fault of her own she has had a terrible injury.*
> Then: *she's actually done really well. No-one thought she would survive. She has a lot of potential. She's so young.*
> Therefore: *I find I really put a lot into Angelica. I just want to examine absolutely all possible opportunities to help her improve.*

Michelle views Angelica as 'deserving' of additional therapy input because she is perceived as having potential. The potential is related primarily to her age and the therapist's belief that because Angelica has so many more years to live, the quality of her performance is important to her quality of life. Contrast this position with Michelle's views on another patient – an elderly man whose clinical picture is consistent with Angelica's.

> Given that: *I think a little more treatment will do him good. I think he deserves it. They need support as a family, they need reassurance. I think people deserve a chance to improve if they can . . .*
> Then: *however, there is a limit to that . . . it's not something I can keep doing . . .*
> Therefore: *like now, after ten weeks I'm thinking it would be better if we stopped . . .*

In her reasoning about this man, Michelle still posits a personal belief that quality of life is important and that people should be given a chance to improve through therapy. The extent of treatment given is still based on her perceptions of whether a patient is 'deserving' or not. Acceptable quality of life for this older man, however, is viewed by Michelle as being 'looked after' by his family and his treatment is considerably shorter than Angelica's. Using the model outlined in Figure 3.5 to explain Michelle's thinking, the following can be hypothesised.

Michelle articulates a set of beliefs about what is ethical (people deserve a chance to improve; younger people deserve more of a chance). These beliefs lead to a set of personal norms that relate to occupational therapy intervention and include specific values about the quality of life that is acceptable at different ages. The personal norms generate an intention to provide therapy in a certain way and for a specific length of time (long term or short term) based on the age of the patient. The result in terms of therapy is a difference in the final form of therapy offered – long term for 18-year-old Angelica (more chance to recover) and short term for the older man (less chance to recover). The fact that there was a difference between occupational therapy offered to the two clients did not pose an ethical problem for Michelle as it mirrored her own set of personal norms and was therefore considered acceptable by her.

PERSONAL BELIEFS RELATED TO FAITH AND HOPE FOR THE FUTURE

Both Diane and Michelle articulated strong beliefs that related to their faith and hope for a positive future for Angelica. For example, in part of Diane's narrative, her strong belief in a better future (recovery) for Angelica determined her own expectations of therapy.

> **Given that:** *my expectations were a lot higher than what I got. But then, I do that with all my patients. I expect them to get better . . . otherwise I wouldn't be treating them . . .*

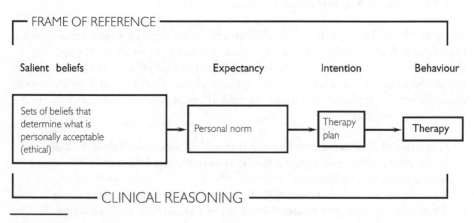

Figure 3.5

Personal beliefs, personal norms and clinical reasoning.

Then: *don't ask me why . . . I had a dream that one day she woke up and spoke to me . . . Looking in her eyes . . . I thought she was going to be better than she was . . . I thought she was more aware . . .*

Therefore: *so I . . . (she gives a list of what she has done with Angelica over the last month) . . . I just have to exhaust all my resources . . .*

Despite Angelica's severe brain impairment, Diane held a strong belief (faith and hope) that she would improve. Over the course of the weeks, Diane was observed treating Angelica every day, sometimes twice a day, trying many different approaches. Angelica was eventually discharged home. Diane was asked: 'At what point did you decide that she wasn't going to get as good as you hoped?' Diane's response demonstrated the same hypothetico–deductive thinking process as described before.

Given that: *. . . after about three or four months . . . we had been treating her twice a day and she hadn't improved over that time . . . we tried everything . . . I thought 'she's not getting better . . .'*

Then: *it's either going to take more time . . . or she's going to be like this forever . . .*

Therefore: *she'll go home for a while and then come back again to rehab when her family need respite and we'll try again . . .*

The therapist generates two possible reasons for the client's lack of response. She tentatively explores the option that Angelica is never going to 'get better'. Her plan is still based on hope that there will be recovery as she plans to see her again in the future for more therapy. Despite weeks of work without much gain, when asked 'What if someone else like Angelica came in now and you had to treat her?', her answer reflected her continued personal belief that 'people get better'.

I would probably do all the same things . . . nobody can predict . . . I think people need a chance . . . at least they deserve a chance of you exhausting all your resources before you give up . . . it's not a waste of time.

and finally:

. . . if I didn't believe that, I couldn't treat Angelica.

Diane used her personal knowledge, specifically her personal beliefs relating to her faith or 'knowing' that 'things get better' in the future. These strong beliefs generate an intention (therapy plan) that incorporates giving the same options to a person with poor prognosis and little potential as to a person who is perceived as having 'better potential'. Diane's expectations for the outcome of therapy are therefore predictably high for Angelica. The resulting therapy is a course of intervention that is just as intense for each client, despite the perceived prognosis. Although she wasn't able to achieve the expected outcomes for Angelica, Diane did fulfil her own expectations by 'exhausting all her resources'. Therapy, therefore, was not perceived by her as having 'failed', as evidenced by her closing statements:

I was happy with what I did . . . I'd do the same again . . .

THINKING 'ABOUT' AND THINKING 'THAT'

So far in this chapter, elements of a hypothesised internal therapist reality have been studied and causative links demonstrated between sets of beliefs, reasoning and therapy. From the perspective of attitude–behaviour theory, reasoning can be described as the constant reconciliation of the actual (*therapy*) and the possible (*intention*). In studying the narratives from this session, two aspects of thinking were apparent: thinking 'about' and thinking 'that'. Thinking 'about' was descriptive and held qualities of Mattingly's narrative reasoning (Mattingly and Fleming, 1994). Thinking 'that' contained more propositional thinking. They were not, however, dichotomous ways of thinking. When the therapists engaged in thinking 'about', there was little propositional thinking but instead, a rich description of every element of the treatment. For example, here's what Diane said:

Well! I thought that was really quite good. Sometimes she will look and try to reach . . . people with brain injury do that – it's inconsistent. I started off with the first bit – that rolling stuff. I'd forgotten about her catheter!!!! She likes that. I thought it was great how she tried to reach the switch. She turned over . . . and then when we'd all had enough of that . . . (she kept describing the session in detail).

This thinking 'about' was conscious thought. It was continuous. Diane made choices about what she was going to think about. She contextualised the treatment event by relating the present to the past, the particular client to all people with brain injury. Thinking 'about' contained a time-gap quality whereby Diane's here-and-now thinking was connected to her past realities of Angelica and all 'Angelicas' she had treated.

This thinking 'about' appeared to form a precondition for therapists to formulate propositions in a more elaborate and focused way. As their narrative progressed, the therapists' thinking turned into more thinking 'that'. Thinking 'that' contained the propositional episodes outlined throughout this chapter and consisted of the '*given that*', '*then*' and '*therefore*' elements of thinking. The relationship between the two is conceptualised in terms of a dynamic system which was sometimes, but not always, linear. Both therapists flowed easily between thinking 'about' (preconditional thinking) and thinking 'that' (propositional thinking) along the continuum of funnelling their thoughts towards a conclusion. The relationship between this preconditional type of thought, hypothetico–deductive thinking and making conclusions about action is pictured in Figure 3.6.

As shown in Figure 3.6, there is an evaluative feedback loop from any action which served to: reinforce decisions that were made during the reasoning process;

Figure 3.6

Thinking 'about' and thinking 'that': the inductive–hypothetico–deductive thinking continuum.

stimulate continuous hypothetico–deductive reasoning as treatment proceeded; and provide an additional source of inductive input that assisted therapists to monitor their own actions. The link between aspects of the continuous inductive–hypothetico–deductive reasoning process and the elements already described in this chapter is hypothesised in Figure 3.1.

SUMMARY

This chapter has shown that multiple decisions are made about the course of therapy in one treatment session and that the capability for purposive therapist action is rooted in thinking. Therapy performance is conceptually represented in the present, but conceived future states are converted into current motivators and regulators of therapy behaviours. In this functional explanation of the relationship between clinical reasoning and actual therapy, therapists act for the sake of realising a particular set of goals. These therapy goals are not realised independently of thought. They are the product of forethought, or reasoning, which is translated into incentives and courses of action. Therapists form beliefs about what they can do, what they are expected to do and what they want to do. Based on these beliefs they anticipate likely positive and negative outcomes of a variety of different options and plan a course of action designed to realise desired futures and avoid others. Beliefs that are salient to one moment in time and the attitudes derived from those beliefs play a central causative role in the reasoning of therapists.

Fleming (1991; Mattingly and Fleming, 1994) has proposed the notion of a therapist with a three-track mind. It is unclear, however, whether Fleming is describing *what* therapists think about that is different or whether *how* therapists think in situations is different. Diane and Michelle have demonstrated that therapists think 'about' more than three things; therefore, from the perspective of thought content, therapists potentially have a 'five-track mind'. When treating Angelica, Diane and Michelle thought about:

1 illness, diagnosis and disability;
2 the whole client/carer situation;
3 the therapy context and environment;
4 their own personal beliefs and expectations of therapy;

5 the degree to which they felt they were able to actualise what needed to be done.

Moreover, any one of these 'tracks' had the potential to influence decision making. Supporting previous findings by Chapparo (1997), narratives of these therapists demonstrate a multidimensional inductive–hypothetical–deductive reasoning style. Whereas the therapists considered multiple elements of thought *content*, they used mainly one *mode* of thinking to make decisions about therapy. This one mode of thinking had the potential to draw together very disparate areas of thought, such as personal–emotional, contextual rules of operation, client needs and science, into a coherent, integrated judgement about the course of action in therapy.

Schwartz (1991) proposed that there were multiple reasoning forms of intelligence and describes how therapists have different ways of 'knowing'. The two therapists studied in this treatment session also demonstrated different ways of 'knowing'; that is, they had different realities and came to different conclusions about what was 'real'. The theory of planned behaviour and its derivatives were used to demonstrate how these two therapists thought about many things, but arrived at a variety of different conclusions using the same basic process of thinking. The process as described in this chapter is not a slow, detached problem-solving process (Dreyfus and Dreyfus, 1986). Using the theory of planned behaviour, this chapter has shown that an inductive–hypothetico–deductive mode of thinking is a highly personal style of thinking that has, as just one of its strands, an examination of facts and, as another, an emotive element. If only one of the elements of thinking is examined, for example, thinking about the client, the thinking appears confused and fragmentary, as described by Fleming (1994). If all elements are considered relative to a given therapist's action at any one time, the process can be seen to blend seemingly fragmented pieces of thought together in a way that funnels thinking towards a conclusion.

Rogers (1983) and others (Sarbin, Taft and Bailey, 1960) have stated that interpretation of the client's situation relative to the therapist's own perspective is reasoning error. Occupational therapy literature suggests that there is a 'right' way and a 'wrong' way to reason. Using the theory of planned behaviour to explain reasoning prompts us to question whether it is possible for occupational therapy, beyond identifying disease signs and symptoms, to have a right and a wrong way of thinking. Within this model, the concept of 'correctness' is highly personal. A common commitment to what is 'right' and 'wrong' in therapy decision making is perhaps not possible. Each therapy event studied in this treatment session generated decisions for action that were made on a broad range of individual sets of beliefs. It is inconceivable to consider the concept of 'right' and 'wrong' without first identifying a set standard. The error standard, as demonstrated by the therapists in just one treatment session, constituted a decision for their own action that was made against a personally acceptable standard. This standard changed from therapist to therapist and from one clinical event to another. There was no common ground defined by both therapists or by all therapy events, only each therapist's own reality of perceived 'good' and 'bad', 'acceptable' or 'unacceptable'.

Within each therapist's own personal reality, the thinking process outlined in this chapter can be described as the therapist's own action turned in on itself. Of paramount importance to the therapist was her own actions – 'What will I do?'. Although the client, the client's mother and context played key roles in the motivation for the therapists to act in a certain way, their own actions remained the pivotal concern of thinking. Therapist thinking therefore focused on the therapy itself; examining its purposes, examining its conditions, considering its resources and difficulties and identifying its obstructions.

Further thoughts

1 Think of a client with whom you are working. Using the theory of planned behaviour, identify the 'given that', the 'then' and the 'therefore' and plan your next treatment session.
2 Thinking about your own workplace or fieldwork experiences, discuss your own personal reality and the implications for how you work as a therapist.
3 Video is used by Diane and Michelle to reflect on their practice. What methods could you use to give you a deeper understanding of your clients and your ways of working with them?

REFERENCES

Ajzen, I. (1985) From intentions to actions: a theory of planned behaviours. In J. Kuhl and J. Beckman (eds) *Action Control: From Cognition to Behaviour.* Springer, Heidelberg.

Ajzen, I., Madden, T. J. (1986) Prediction of goal directed behaviour: attitudes, intentions and perceived behavioural control. *Journal of Experimental Social Psychology*, 5, 400–416.

Bridge, C., Twible, R. (1997) Clinical reasoning: informed decision making for practice. In C. Christiansen and C. Baum (eds) *Enabling Function and Well Being*, 2nd edn. Slack, Thorofare, NJ, pp. 158–179.

Chapparo, C. (1997) Influences on clinical reasoning in occupational therapy. Unpublished PhD thesis, School of Education, Macquarie University, Ryde, NSW, Australia.

Chapparo, C., Ranka, J. (1995) Clinical reasoning in occupational therapy. In J. Higgs and M. Jones (eds) *Clinical Reasoning in the Health Professions.* Butterworth Heinemann, London.

Christiansen, C., Baum, C. (eds) (1997) *Enabling Function and Well Being.* 2nd edn. Slack, Thorofare, NJ.

Dreyfus, H. Dreyfus, S. (1986) *Mind over Machine. The Power of Human Intuition and Expertise in the Era of the Computer.* Free Press, New York.

Dutton, R. (1995) *Clinical Reasoning in Physical Disabilities.* Williams and Wilkins, Baltimore.

Fleming, M. H. (1991) The therapist with a three track mind. *American Journal of Occupational Therapy*, 45(11), 1007–1014.

Fleming, M. H. (1994) Procedural reasoning: addressing functional limitations. In C. Mattingly and M. H. Fleming (eds) *Clinical Reasoning: Forms of Inquiry in a Therapeutic Practice*. F. A. Davis, Philadelphia.

Higgs, J., Jones, M. (eds) (1995) *Clinical Reasoning in the Health Professions*. Butterworth Heinemann, London.

Kovich, K., Bermann, D. E. (1988) *Head Injury: A Guide to Functional Outcomes in Occupational Therapy*. Aspen Publications, Gaithersburg, Maryland.

Mattingly, C., Fleming, M. H. (1994) *Clinical Reasoning: Forms of Inquiry in a Therapeutic Practice*. F. A. Davis, Philadelphia.

Parham, D. (1987) Toward professionalism: the reflective therapist. *American Journal of Occupational Therapy*, 41(9), 555–561.

Polanyi, M. (1966) *Personal Knowledge*. Routledge and Kegan Paul, London.

Rogers, J. C. (1983) Eleanor Clarke Slagle Lectureship 1983. Clinical reasoning: the ethics, science and art. *American Journal of Occupational Therapy*, 37(9), 601–616.

Rogers, J. C. (1986) Clinical judgement: the bridge between theory and practice. In AOTA, *Target 2000: Occupational Therapy Education*. American Occupational Therapy Association, Rockville, MD.

Sarbin, T. R., Taft, R., and Bailey, D. E. (1960) *Clinical Inference and Cognitive Theory*. Holt, Rinehart and Winston, New York.

Schell, B. A., Cervero, R. M. (1993) Clinical reasoning in occupational therapy: an integrative review. *American Journal of Occupational Therapy*, 47, 605–610.

Schon, D. (1987) *Educating the Reflective Practitioner*. Jossey-Bass, San Francisco.

Schwartz, K. B. (1991) Clinical reasoning and new ideas on intelligence: implications for teaching and learning. *American Journal of Occupational Therapy*, 45(11), 1033–1037.

Ylvisaker, M. (1985) *Head Injury Rehabilitation*. Taylor and Francis, London.

SECTION TWO _____

DESCRIBING PRACTICE

4 LILLIAN AND PAULA: A TREATMENT NARRATIVE IN ACUTE MENTAL HEALTH

Elizabeth Anne McKay

KEY POINTS
- Initial images and revised images
- Engagement
- Phenomenological perspectives
- Clinical reasoning model for acute mental health

Clinical reasoning in the mental health arena has received little attention to date so this chapter could be a useful starting point. It highlights that within this setting the therapist continued to build and alter her initial image of the client through the process of treatment. Pattern recognition, cues and the therapist's past experience all played a part in her way of working. Cues and patterns may not be as obvious in mental health as in other occupational therapy practice areas. This study reinforces the author's belief that the client should be at the core of therapy.

This chapter will tell the story of a therapist and one of her clients. First, the scene will be set and the two main characters introduced, then their joint story of therapy told. The chapter will finish by discussing the implications for practice for both learners and practitioners. All names have been altered to maintain anonymity for those involved.

SETTING THE SCENE

This story is just one of many stories that unfolded as I collected data for my MSc research. It began when I arrived at the general hospital on the first day to begin the data collection phase. It was August 14th and I had driven the 50-mile journey in bright clear sunshine under a cloudless blue sky. As it was such a beautiful day I felt more like I was going on holiday. Once into the hospital building I was immediately aware of the sudden change from light to dark; the walls inside the building were various shades of brown and russets, very 1970s, and very dark in contrast to the bright sunlight I had just left. It seemed to reflect my research question! I was trying to shed light on a therapist's way of thinking and her way of working through her decisions with her clients and this seemed an appropriate metaphor for the study: the interplay between light and dark, the known and unknown.

The actors

Lillian, the occupational therapist

Lillian had worked in this acute mental health ward for just over a year, having recently returned to her occupational therapy career. Her past occupational therapy experience had included working in several psychiatric teaching hospitals in Britain. Lillian then worked as the manager of an occupational therapy service before, latterly, taking up a lecturing post.

Although she was away from the profession while involved with her family, she had several related jobs: lecturing in a local college, working with women who wished to change or start new careers and also as a marriage guidance counsellor. During this time she completed a degree in social sciences.

Within this unit, Lillian had responsibility for working with people from one of the two acute psychiatry wards of a district general hospital. The hospital covered a large geographical area and had within its boundaries urban and rural communities. Both Lillian and her colleague Nancy worked together on several occasions during each week, co-facilitating group treatment sessions for each other. In a normal week, Lillian would be involved in working both with groups of clients and with individuals. She was actively involved with people who had recently returned home after an admission to the ward and was interested in offering support to bridge the move from hospital to home.

Lillian had agreed to take part in my study several months before. She and I had met previously to look at her normal working week and to get to know each other. We had agreed that I would be working alongside her for two weeks, observing and interviewing on a daily basis. On her return to work after a holiday, Lillian made her first contact with the client on whose story we will focus.

Paula, the client

Paula was a woman in her late 40s. Prior to this admission, Paula had lived at home with her husband and her son. Paula's daughter, who had her own child, had left home but she kept in regular contact with her mother, and Paula enjoyed being a grandmother. Over the years she had had several previous admissions to the psychiatric hospital. She had spent some time on the ward the previous year and since then she had been attending a local mental health day unit. However, her attendance was sporadic and she had failed to attend for several consultant appointments in the recent past. Lillian and Paula had not met before.

Act 1 – first meeting

The story of Lillian and Paula began on the Monday morning of Lillian's return to work. At the morning case review, Lillian was made aware of a new female patient, Paula, who had been admitted to the ward over the weekend. Lillian was told by the nursing staff that Paula had been found wandering on a railway line and this had resulted in Paula's admission to the ward. Lillian was made aware of Paula's recent home circumstances. Her son had been a victim of abuse by a neighbour and as a result this neighbour was currently serving a prison sentence. This had caused much distress in the household and Social Services were still involved with the family.

Before meeting with Paula, I asked Lillian what initial image she had of Paula and what she expected to see on meeting her. From the information given at the case review, Lillian had built a picture of a depressed woman; she linked this to the apparent suicidal behaviour of Paula walking on the railway line. She thought she might see someone who was perhaps unable to assert herself and therefore unable to cope or keep her son safe. Lillian expected to see a woman who was 'vulnerable and one of life's victims'.

Lillian arranged to meet with Paula later in the morning, to get to know her and to find out what her needs and wishes were and in what way, if any, occupational therapy could help to meet those needs. Paula was asked if it would be all right for me to come along with Lillian. She agreed.

However, on meeting Paula a different picture emerged. The image Lillian had constructed proved to be incorrect. Paula presented as neither clinically depressed nor vulnerable. She was a tall, well-built woman with significant presence. However, what did become clear from this first meeting was that Paula was having difficulty with Lillian's questions. As I observed, Lillian quickly changed her style of questioning, repeating and reframing questions for Paula, giving her clear uncluttered questions to help her to understand them. It seemed that Paula was slow intellectually, an area not known or considered by Lillian before their meeting. As a result of this new awareness, Lillian then monitored the pace of the interview, allowing Paula more time to reply. Lillian asked open questions to elicit further information from Paula. As Paula changed the direction of the conversation, Lillian continued easily along the new route. It appeared to me that Lillian tuned into Paula's conversation, listening actively to what she was saying. Lillian encouraged Paula to describe her own situation.

Lillian: *I gather you were feeling the same this time going down to the railway track, why were you feeling so bad?*
Paula: *I wanted to end it all.*
Lillian: *Did you feel rather hopeless?*
Paula: *I've not seen my son.*
Lillian: *Is he out of touch at the moment? He'll be worrying about you.*

As the interview continued it became clear that Paula felt that she had lost some of her role within the family. She said her husband had taken over some of her tasks within the home, like the cooking, and Paula seemed sad that she no longer had this role. As Paula talked about her home it became clear that her relationship with her husband also appeared strained and it was obvious that she felt unable to ask for his help. As Lillian said:

She was worried about phoning him, even to say, when you are coming (to visit), could you bring my glasses?

Following this meeting I asked Lillian for her thoughts. Lillian acknowledged that she had changed her initial image of Paula. Throughout this meeting Lillian felt she continued to revise and build onto her present picture of Paula and her current life. She also expressed her awareness that during this meeting she was revisiting her past knowledge, especially in relation to learning theory. She recalled that she had read somewhere that 'questions should not be any more difficult than for a seven-year-old to understand'. She was trying to enhance her ability to communicate successfully with Paula, to make the first meeting useful so that their future work together could be positive.

ACT 2 – WORKING TOGETHER

Over the next two weeks these two women worked together with a view to Paula being discharged home as soon as possible. I would like to present some of their shared story. Lillian, in planning her intervention with Paula, highlighted two important aspects that would form a basis for her treatment relationship with Paula. First, she would have to work at Paula's level of functioning and she suspected that Paula overestimated her ability. Second, she would need to work with what Paula identified as being relevant and important to her.

During the course of their first meeting Paula had expressed interest in a range of activities and her treatment programme reflected these. It included the walking group, craft work and individual time for kitchen and computing work. Straight away, Lillian chose to follow a practical approach. She hoped this would allow Paula to experience success in treatment and by so doing, increase her self-esteem, her self-confidence and her motivation to continue to work towards her discharge home.

With regard to the diagnosis of depression, Lillian felt that there were no overt depressive symptoms. Although she recognised that Paula was in need of care and attention, Lillian felt that Paula had few ways of talking about her distress, hence the 'walk on the railway line'. Lillian believed that Paula was stressed by the events around her and that she felt she had no control over these. She needed respite from her home situation and an environment which made her feel safe, secure and valued.

It became clear to me from talking to Lillian that, in developing her initial feel for Paula, she worked to a mental checklist. She used this as a framework to build her understanding of Paula. This checklist focused on Paula's relationships, her roles, routines and strengths and any recent changes to any or all of these areas. As she worked with Paula, she was simultaneously considering Paula's situation and examining ways in which occupational therapy could match these needs. This process took place not only within the initial meeting but throughout their time working together. As I observed her with other clients, she seemed to follow the same process. It appeared that this mental checklist could be considered as a personal template for matching client needs to therapy. However, I thought that Lillian was not always aware of this process taking place.

Lillian continued to examine her client's situation by exploring 'roles and relationships'. She felt that Paula's usual roles within the family were significantly reduced or lost to the extent that the sick role was becoming dominant. This change had a destabilising effect on Paula and in her case could have been significant in her admission to the hospital. Therefore, in developing a treatment programme, Lillian worked to stabilise and improve Paula's normal range of roles. Paula's treatment programme reflected this need to recapture previous roles within the family. One of her most significant losses was her role in the home around meal preparation. This loss had not been positive from Paula's point of view. Therefore opportunities were included in the treatment programme to regain confidence around this valued role in baking and cooking sessions. Interestingly, Lillian spoke of a 'woman's place not necessarily being in the home' but for Paula this was a valued role she had lost and therefore the opportunity to develop and regain confidence and skills was important to her.

During this work, Lillian emphasised the need for treatment to be relevant and important to the individual. She felt she had to engage Paula in the intervention but at the same time allow her to retain her personal autonomy. This notion of 'positive engagement' was used by Lillian to engage all her clients in their treatment experience. It included choice of and relevance of treatment and the valuing and supporting of clients. Lillian believed that clients should be given options and opportunities by involvement in decision making regarding their own treatment, however small these decisions were. This was illustrated when Paula was working on the computer. It was evident from her level of functioning that she had little skill with the computer, although she stated that previously she had been to classes. Nonetheless, she had an interest in using it.

Lillian: *Can you tell me what you've done before (on the computer)?*
Paula: *I've done letters.*
Lillian: *Did you write letters?*
Paula: *Yes.*
Lillian: *Is there anyone you'd like to write to just now?*
Paula: *My granddaughter.*
Lillian: *Would you like to write it out first?*
Paula: *Yes.*
Lillian: *I'll pop in and out every so often to see how you're doing.*

Here the therapist taps into an area of interest to maintain her client's motivation by enabling her to experience success and have a positive valued outcome, which was communication with her granddaughter. Paula's skills with the computer were few but with Lillian's help she persisted and compiled a letter to her granddaughter which she was desperate to post. Lillian summed it up well:

I think a lot you do with a patient is relevant if you've discussed it with them and agree that it's related to some kind of function they are struggling with.

Lillian demonstrated as she worked with Paula that she valued her as a person in her own right, reinforcing the importance of self. Lillian felt strongly that Paula would not benefit from a 'hands off' approach, as she judged that such an approach would lead to failure, increasing Paula's anxiety. She chose to work alongside Paula, taking a companionship role, as they worked together in the kitchen. Whilst cooking, she worked at her side offering practical help, hoping that this would alleviate Paula's stress. This approach as 'coach' was further encouraged by Lillian's openness to 'make connections' with Paula. This process of making connections was a way of 'hooking in' the client: getting their interest or involvement by creating external motivation for the client. With Paula, this involved Lillian disclosing some of her own personal life to Paula in an exchange during the cooking of a meal.

> Paula: *Do you have any children?*
> Lillian: *Yes, three.*
> Paula: *Three boys?*
> Lillian: *No, one boy, two girls, he's sandwiched between them.*
> Paula: *My daughter is 23.*

Here, there is common ground on which the two women can exchange their stories and life experiences and therefore come together. Schwartzberg (1993) cites Sperber (1989) who identified self-disclosure as one method used by therapists to create a partnership with clients.

Another way in which Lillian built connections with Paula was by her use of humour. She put Paula at ease by telling of her own cooking disasters, helping to reduce tension. This also had the effect of levelling the relationship: instead of therapist and patient, they became two women who at times had culinary disasters. Lillian reflected that she was aware that she used humour as a bridge to build relationships; it enabled her to be seen on equal terms with her clients. She was also aware that humour used inappropriately could be a barrier to effective working. Vergeer and MacRae (1993) identified from their qualitative research 16 themes with regard to the use of humour by occupational therapists. The importance of humour in creating an equal and collaborative relationship between the client and the therapist was highlighted. Humour can be used to set the right tone for the relationship, promoting a client-centred approach.

At the time of my leaving the unit, Paula was due to return home for weekend leave which was a major step for her future. From Paula's and other stories, I would like to propose a clinical reasoning model for occupational therapy in mental health. The model is derived from the therapist's implicit way of working and decision making based on the findings from the study.

ACT 3 – A CLINICAL REASONING MODEL

This model proposes that the therapist's clinical reasoning processes are informed and constructed by four key components: the working environment, the client, the therapeutic context and, importantly, the therapist. These components can be separated from each other. However, they all need to be taken into account to enable the therapist to construct her image of the client and the resultant treatment response.

The working environment

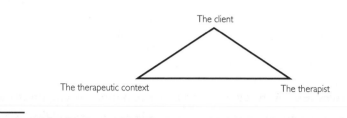

Figure 4.1

A clinical reasoning model.

Working environment

The working environment is any setting in which a therapist works. This environment informs the therapist's reasoning processes in several ways. It sites the therapist's work within given boundaries, in which certain other factors exist. These factors may include facilities, staffing roles, modes of operation by team members, availability of resources, local policies and procedures and the political views of the moment. All these impact on the therapist's reasoning processes. The environment, although dynamic and susceptible to change, remains nonetheless relatively stable. Included within the working environment are staff members from a variety of backgrounds who provide a range of services. Multidisciplinary issues arise as a result of different staff working together, often with different foci. For this occupational therapist, one issue was the role she played in the service. This role may require negotiation with others and may place overt or covert boundaries on the therapist's way of working.

Merton (1968) and Goffman (1969) have defined and developed the concept of 'role'. They have made much of 'role' as performance, arguing that each of us plays a number of roles in relation to different situations. Lillian had roles that placed certain expectations on how she performed. Within her working environment, she had roles as a team member, administrator, professional and helper. Schon (1983) acknowledges that 'All professional roles are embedded in the institutional context'. This context bounds the scope of practice, enabling the practitioner to build a repertoire of examples, facts and experiences. How the therapist met the demands and expectations of these myriad roles impacted on how she thought and functioned within this environment. Therefore this working environment provided the backdrop in which the therapist worked with clients.

The client

The client is considered as being multifaceted and the therapist, Lillian, sought to build an image of the client, Paula, by exploring and understanding these facets. The therapist developed an initial sense of her client; she identified that she built her sense of the client from whatever data were available. This initial sensing led to assumptions that may or may not be disregarded as the therapist worked with the client over time. These initial assumptions, if not reflected on, could colour future involvement and lead to a less valid treatment programme being implemented. As new information is assimilated, the therapist endeavours to understand the client and their particular life situation. This is achieved by taking a *Gestalt* view of the client. Lillian did this by building a picture of the client, from her own past experiences of other clients, her considerable knowledge base, from cues from the client and other sources and by recognition and interpretation of patterns. These all informed Lillian's interpretation of her understanding of Paula and played a part in how she reasoned and the treatment decisions she took.

Mostly, this occurred at a subconscious level, which Schon (1983) termed 'reflection-in-action'. However, at times Lillian was consciously aware of particular pattern matching occurring. These included the diagnosis as well as psychological, social and cultural patterns. Here, recognitions seemed to be related to the therapist recognising similarities between past clients, their signs, symptoms and their situations and matching these to her current client situations. Munroe (1992) cites Norman and Tugwell (1985) who concluded that consistency in clinical problem solving relied less on theoretical knowledge than on the capacity of the practitioner to tap into an extensive store of experiential knowledge. To recognise patterns, it is necessary for the practitioner to have experienced them previously.

Another important aspect of the client was 'roles and relationships'. The therapist continued to examine the client's situation by exploring her roles and relationships. The therapist identified that roles within the family were significantly reduced or lost and that the 'sick' role could become dominant. With Paula, this loss of role had a destabilising effect. The complexity of family relationships and situations also became a focus for Lillian when developing understanding of her clients. She believed that individuals need to be viewed within their own context and not be seen as separate from it.

When considering the client, Lillian paid attention to diagnosis and medication but only to inform her understanding of the client. Lillian felt strongly that you had to see the 'individual' rather than their diagnosis or medication.

The therapeutic context

The third key component of the model is the therapeutic context. This area deals with the setting in which treatment or treatment-related activities take place. It encompasses therapist/client interactions as these give meaning to the experience for the client and therapist. The context is set within the working environment but can be considered as separate from it. An activity would normally form part of the interaction. Central to the therapeutic context is the communication, both verbal and non-verbal, between the therapist and client. Especially important is the way the spoken word is used. It is the language of the therapist which values, encourages and offers the possibility of change to the client. It is this within the context of treatment that gives meaning to the experience for both the client and the therapist. Integral to therapeutic context are the concepts of 'temporal perspectives' and the 'creation of conducive climates'.

Temporal perspectives encapsulate time, considered by the therapist as the 'here and now' and the future. Knowing the 'right' time was important; this included the right time to get involved, the right time to change approach and the right time to withdraw from the treatment process. This notion needs sensitivity towards the emotional needs of a particular client.

Another important aspect is 'creating conducive climates', involving those factors that enhance the client's treatment experience. These were to the forefront in the therapist's thinking as she worked to produce a climate that facilitated effective intervention. The therapist aimed to produce safe and secure treatment, thereby providing non-threatening sessions which would encourage participation. The context is ever changing, it is powerful and it may influence or alter the therapist's understanding of the client.

The therapist

The final area of the proposed model to be considered is the concept of the 'therapist'. Within this study Lillian made decisions and performed in the light of past experience and current knowledge and skills. She believed in the potential of occupational therapy. She worked to engage the client and create a climate for successful treatment. This influenced how she interpreted information from the other three components of the model by acting as a filter, thereby creating her own image of the client. The therapist can mould treatment intervention to create change for clients. Key aspects of this area included the notions of 'productivity and participation', 'positive engagement' and lastly 'private and professional self'. These are explained below.

First, 'productivity and participation' concerned the therapist's view of occupational therapy which she perceived as being positive and valuable to clients. She believed that her clients benefited from participating in treatment. For some, this may have included the production of an end-product; for others, it was actively taking part in a process, for example a group walk. She believed that occupational therapy had a unique perspective to offer clients. Second, 'positive engagement' deals with the strategies used by the therapist to engage clients in the treatment experience. It included choice of and relevance of treatment, valuing and supporting clients. Lillian believed that you needed to work on areas clients identified as being important as this increased their motivation to engage in the treatment whilst encouraging them to maintain their personal autonomy. Making connections helped the therapist to make links with clients to gain their participation.

The final concept of the therapist is 'private and professional self'. This considered both internal and external factors which influenced Lillian such as her past life experiences, knowledge, beliefs, values and current skills. She was aware of her preferred ways of working. She identified that she followed the occupational therapy department's commitment to client-centred practice. The therapist was aware of her own skills and expertise changing over time and she felt more able to deal with uncertainty in practice, thus supporting Dreyfus' (1979) view that professionals do not base their decisions on rules. For example, Lillian's reason for not looking at case notes prior to seeing clients was that she felt able to deal with the client's situation as it presented. How this model may be used to assist occupational therapists and students to articulate their practice will be considered in the next section.

IMPLICATIONS FOR PRACTICE

In light of the findings within this acute mental health setting, it is proposed that as the occupational therapist worked with clients, she constructed images of them. Her reasoning in relation to the client was influenced by the working environment, the therapeutic context and what she herself brought personally and professionally to the setting. The proposed model offers both the learner and practising therapist a framework in which they could begin to isolate and identify how a therapist clinically reasons. The learner could focus on the four key components and use these to guide and structure questions in the right area. Questions should be reflective, addressing how and why. The questioning needs to span a continuum from factual knowledge to critical analysis of the situation. Similarly, the therapist should pose reflective questions to learners, using the model to facilitate students' verbalisation of their thoughts on their actions from an early stage.

These findings suggest that a more phenomenological perspective for developing reasoning should be encouraged. Learners and therapists should seek to broaden their view of clients. For instance they should try to consider what it is like to suffer from depression rather than just learning signs, symptoms or techniques. Within this study medication and diagnosis were acknowledged but these in no way drove the therapist's reasoning processes.

To this end, a more expansive view of the client is required. The use of materials such as those described below would encourage different perspectives to be utilised. For example, literature and film, both fact and fiction, which portray different life experiences should be encouraged. Peloquin (1989) stresses that the use of such resources provides occupational therapists with 'images of relationships and images of qualities that make relationships meaningful'. Murray (1997) advocates the use of medical humanities to encourage reflection by therapists to understand about clients' experiences of health and social care.

Within the academic setting, there is a need for learners to be exposed to real people, simulated events and lastly paper case stories, in that order, as this exposure allows students to construct more indepth images of clients, building up their own repertoire of clinical pictures. Neistadt (1987) advocated using former clients within the classroom. The use of video of clients and therapists with expert analysis would encourage the verbalisation of reasoning processes within a safe environment. Burke and Depoy (1991) suggest that 'guided observation with master clinicians' is one way of assisting learners to recognise patterns and meanings in a given situation. Therapists should be encouraged to share their clinical stories with each other, widening their memory (library) of experiences and thereby increasing the range of examples and the likelihood of pattern recognition in the future. McKay and Ryan (1995) propose that sharing personal and professional stories allows students to practise describing and explaining their involvement with clients. Within all these ways of developing reasoning, verbalisation of stories and what is underpinning them is crucial.

SUMMARY

The story, the model and the implications for practice presented here emerged from my MSc study. The findings confirmed some things I had experienced both as a therapist and as a fieldwork educator working with learners. The complexity of information and the variety of processes used by the therapist to make sense of her clients and her ways of working with clients were surprising. The finding which was most challenging, yet on reflection was so simple, was the emergence of language and its use within the therapeutic context. This is taken for granted and is assumed to be part of the therapists' abilities. This study highlights the need for the importance of language to be recognised and practised. Finally, this work has been shared with therapists who have demonstrated recognition of the components of the model.

Further thoughts

1 With a colleague, view a short section (5 minutes maximum) of a video which focuses on a person. Write down independently all the cues that you noticed. Compare and discuss these with your colleague. The video does not have to have a medical focus.
2 Thinking of yourself, identify your 'personal and professional self'. Describe it. How do these aspects influence your way of working?
3 Seek out a variety of resources which would broaden your understanding of the clients you work with. How could these be used creatively with a newly qualified therapist or student to enable them to develop a phenomenological perspective of the clients?

REFERENCES

Burke, J., Depoy, E. P. (1991) An emerging view of mastery, excellence and leadership in occupational therapy practice. *American Journal of Occupational Therapy*, 45(11), 1027–1031.
Dreyfus, H. (1979) *What Computers Can't Do*. Harper and Row, New York.
Goffman, E. (1969) *The Presentation of Self in Everyday Life*. Penguin, Harmondsworth.
McKay, E, A., Ryan, S. (1995) Clinical reasoning through story telling: examining a student's case study on a fieldwork placement. *British Journal of Occupational Therapy*, 58(6), 234–238.
Merton, R. (1968) *Social Theory to Social Structure*. Free Press, New York.
Munroe, H. (1992) Clinical reasoning in community occupational therapy: patterns and processes. Unpublished doctoral thesis, Herriot-Watt University, Edinburgh.

Murray, R. (1997) *Ethical Dilemmas in Health Care: A Practical Approach through Medical Humanities*. Stanley Thornes, Cheltenham.

Neistadt, M. E. (1987) Classroom as clinic: a model for teaching clinical reasoning in occupational therapy education. *American Journal of Occupational Therapy*, **41**, 631–677.

Peloquin, S. M. (1989) Sustaining the art of practice in occupational therapy. *American Journal of Occupational Therapy*, **43**(4), 219–227.

Schon, D. (1983) *The Reflective Practitioner: How Professionals Think in Action*. Basic Books, New York.

Schwartzberg, S. L. (1993) Tools of practice, 'therapeutic use of self'. In H. L. Hopkins and H. D. Smith (eds). *Willard and Spackman's Occupational Therapy, 8th edn. J. B. Lippincott, Philadelphia.*

Vergeer, G., MacRae, A. (1993) Therapeutic use of humour in occupational therapy. *American Journal of Occupational Therapy*, 47(8), 678–683.

5 JENNY'S STORY: EXPLORING THE LAYERS OF NARRATIVE REASONING

Rachelle Coe

KEY POINTS
- Working with a young person
- Narrative reasoning: unfolding stories
- Transitional processes
- Team members' stories

One of the interesting aspects of this chapter is how the author has used narrative to present Jenny's story, one being set within the other. The construct of narrative reasoning is discussed and builds on Mattingly's writings on emplotment. Of particular interest is the way the figures presented here aim to visualise the process of the unfolding story. The story plots Jenny's many transitions through the rehabilitation process. The importance of the team members' stories and their differing perspectives is highlighted as significant to working with Jenny and her family.

The following narrative evolved while I was studying a postgraduate module on clinical reasoning. I began to understand my preference for narrative reasoning, as it explained why people always told stories when they were troubled. I had been aware that stories were often used to describe problems and felt this was a way in which I could examine my own clinical issues.

While understanding Mattingly's work on emplotment in narratives, I had difficulty in visualising the role of emplotment in narrative reasoning. Mattingly (1991, 1994a,b) has yet to represent narratives in a visual or model way, her examples to date being based on stories themselves. Perhaps considering a visual model would be viewing narrative from a reductionist or oversimplistic perspective and would devalue the uniqueness of each situation.

Coe (1995) and Medhurst (1996) have tried to view narrative from a cyclical or layered perspective, to attempt to show the connection between the elements of emplotment. The development of layers in a story helps to bring together the images related to each emplotment and ensures that the representation of emplotment continues to have some '3D' qualities and some sense of a developing story.

Mattingly (1991) suggests that stories unwind along a temporal axis and display a wholeness in which each particular episode takes its meaning as part of the larger whole. An interpretation of the concept of emplotment as part of a story is shown in Figure 5.1.

This interpretation developed through my involvement in working with a young girl, Jenny. The stories presented are reflections of events that occurred (names, places and details have been changed to provide anonymity). Jenny's story is a product of my reflection on and interpretation of a series of complex issues and difficulties. It may not reflect the interpretation of the other people involved.

I experienced conflict in my work and thus began to question the role of conflict in rehabilitation. Why do there often seem to be misunderstandings between team members and families? Can we use stories as a method to reduce friction and increase understanding and awareness of others? Can stories be used to help teams plan collaborative practice?

This led to further questioning. What happens to narrative reasoning when the story changes, as a result of medical diagnosis, sudden changes in health status or staff relationships? Why do families tell certain aspects of a story to a therapist? What about the many stories told about certain situations? Does narrative reasoning assist the occupational therapist to practise effectively?

The following narrative reflects the varying and overlapping stories that surfaced while working with Jenny. The chronological aspect of the narrative was pieced together using a framework of emplotment (Mattingly, 1991, 1994b). An incident was examined in detail to highlight the difficulties in working with conflicting stories.

THE NARRATIVE – LAYERS OF STORIES

Setting the scene

I met Jenny when she was transferred from a teaching hospital to the children's ward of the local hospital. She was 12 years old and the eldest child in her family. The children's ward predominately catered for younger children with acute and short-term illnesses. I was asked to work with Jenny as there were no occupational therapists attached to the children's ward.

As a sessional worker at the hospital, I began to notice the different ways in which this large multidisciplinary team worked. The team exchanged information informally, as well as through periodic meetings for professionals and parents.

Chart talk – medical diagnoses

This story begins with Jenny's medical history and the changes in her medical status and diagnoses. I have started the narrative here because this is often the first type of information a therapist is given and the reason a client becomes known to occupational therapy. The specific details of diagnosis are not given as it was thought Jenny was suffering from a rare condition and to indicate further symptoms and terminology could threaten her anonymity.

The cause of Jenny's condition was not known. Her condition had the doctors puzzled, with her diagnosis being altered three or four times, and with these changes

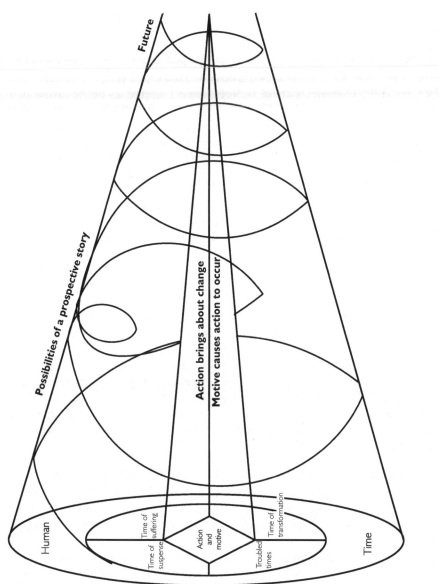

Figure 5.1

Emplotment: moving towards a future story.

came different hospitals. Initially, Jenny was diagnosed with a terminal illness, but further investigations indicated a change of prognosis. Additional difficulties resulted in brain damage and the need for a tracheostomy. Once she was medically stabilised, the staff informed Jenny and her family that she should begin rehabilitation. At this point she was transferred to her local hospital to be close to her family.

The changes in diagnoses were dramatic. While I didn't know the family members when the original diagnosis of terminal illness was given, their emotional reactions may have included sadness, anger and bereavement. With complications to her condition, they may have experienced a loss of hopes and dreams. Perhaps her parents were still experiencing these feelings when I started seeing Jenny, which contributed to them feeling they had 'lost' Jenny's story. With each change in Jenny's narrative, time was needed to determine the possible course of the new story and visions of the future for Jenny, her family and the staff working with them. Figure 5.2 highlights the emplotment at this stage of the story.

Past life story – Jenny's story and her family's story

In order to familiarise myself with Jenny's present abilities, it was important that I discovered more about her past, so I could understand what she used to do and the importance of these occupations. A number of critical or significant incidents occurred prior to her admission to hospital. These included: passing exams for school placement, going to her parents' home country, making a friend, starting high school and undergoing changes related to puberty. After attending high school for a short time, Jenny was admitted to hospital, which gave her little time to meet and make other new friends. Surfacing throughout this story were interlinking ideas and aspects that detailed what her family members were like, for example their goals, values and aspirations. This was in addition to Jenny's place within this framework and her own values, beliefs, interests, hopes and dreams.

Knowing how Jenny perceived the passage of time between her critical incidents increased my understanding of how the experience felt and what it meant to her. Storytelling helped to identify the timing of events that led to the changes that brought Jenny to therapy. She required time to tell her past story and reflect upon it, in order to gain an understanding of the future.

The rehabilitation story – Jenny's story, her family's story and my story

I met Jenny as she was adding another layer to her story – her rehabilitation. I was the new person on the ward's team and I remember being unsure about how the team worked together. I had very few shared stories with the staff, but felt a need to fit into this story.

I was asked to do an assessment of Jenny's occupational therapy needs for rehabilitation. On arrival at the ward, I checked her medical notes to gain some idea of her condition and any restrictions it might imply. For example, with a tracheostomy she probably wouldn't be able to speak. How would I communicate with her? Many questions went through my mind on my way to meet Jenny. Although I wasn't consciously trying to form a physical image of Jenny in my mind, on reflection, the nature of the problems and my lack of hospital experiences probably made image

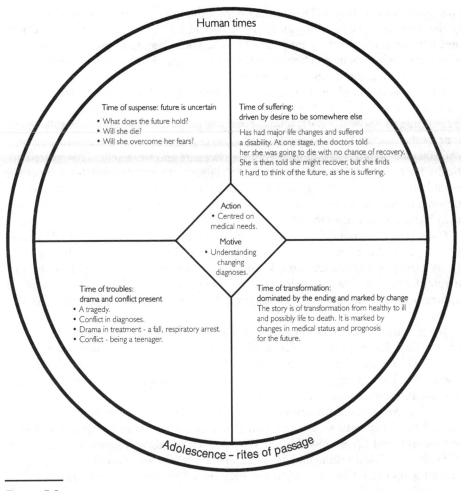

Figure 5.2

Emplotment of Jenny's narrative.

formation difficult for me. The mixed ideas I did have of Jenny had to be revised upon meeting her.

This experience highlights the importance of being aware of the images we form of potential clients and how these images stem from preconceived ideas and assumptions. Ryan (1990) found that novice therapists experienced difficulty in developing these images, as they had little experience on which to base them. They needed to meet the client. If an initial image is not revised, this can result in the professional imposing his or her own values, culture and views on situations.

Jenny presented to me as a very sad, fearful teenager, who was not able to assert herself in any way except by her refusal to move. Staff members on the ward quickly warned me of her 'manipulative behaviour', although I had already seen this noted in the medical records. I imagined what it would be like to be in Jenny's situation and felt that this behaviour may have been her only way to express her emotions, affect her environment and be noticed. If a mismatch of these early images were to remain, misunderstandings would occur.

Jenny was despondent, lonely and confused. She was unsure of how to act or what was expected of her. It was a trying time for those working with her. While she was getting to know the staff, Jenny tested out the boundaries of acceptable behaviour as she reacted by showing dislike for certain members of the team by actively choosing the people she wanted involved in her care and treatment. This created difficulty for staff, as she would often refuse to engage in rehabilitation. Sometimes she would ask that certain family members not to be involved either. Parallels with fiction can be seen here, with certain 'characters' being involved at certain times, with each having roles within the plot.

Gans (1983) highlights the role of conflict and hate as part of the rehabilitation process, describing hate as an expression of powerlessness. This was illustrated in Jenny's story by her refusal to work with certain people as she 'hated' them. Jenny's parents found it difficult to understand their daughter's behaviour, as they no longer understood her and her emotions. Figure 5.3 outlines the story emplotment of this stage.

Jenny feared movement in many forms and refused to participate in physiotherapy sessions. She required the use of a hoist to be transferred. She was also afraid of falling, which was a direct result of having had a fall at a previous hospital. Her fear also seemed to relate to past events, to her successes in education and her fear of failing. She refused to have a wheelchair.

Jenny experienced difficulties which required ongoing occupational therapy. She needed assistance with all tasks of daily living, being unable to mobilise and unsure of how to spend her time within the hospital. Jenny was very concerned about her difficulty with handwriting and its effect on her schoolwork, as well as her difficulty in cutting up food. She was very self-conscious of how she looked to others.

Jenny's occupational therapy programme was based on her priorities and goals to ensure she had some control, meaning and success. Jenny chose to work on her handwriting as she wanted to write letters to others. She became actively involved in her counselling sessions with the psychologist. However, Jenny's involvement in therapy fluctuated and on some days she refused to speak to those working with her.

During this time, the team looked for a more appropriate intensive rehabilitation placement. This created conflict for Jenny, her parents and team members in deciding where she should go and what should happen to her. Jenny found it difficult to accept that she would have to meet a new set of people and be away from her family. Her parents expressed concern over her slow recovery and whether or not they were making the right decision. The team was concerned that the current setting was not geared to long-term intensive rehabilitation. It was difficult to identify whose story the team should listen to. Consequently, decision making appeared very directive and was perhaps not considering all the needs of Jenny and her family.

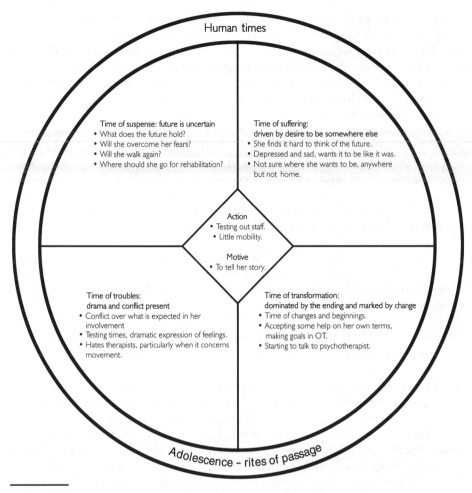

Figure 5.3

Emplotment of Jenny's narrative: rehabilitation story.

With the fear of possibly being transferred to another facility and 'retelling' her story, Jenny became actively involved in treatment. She recognised that she didn't want to move from the hospital but also expressed her anxieties and wishes not to return home. Jenny was also aware that she couldn't return home, as the home environment required extensive modifications. Decisions regarding these modifications hadn't been made at that stage, as it was uncertain what level of support Jenny required, and neither Jenny nor her family were ready to contemplate this future image.

Kielhofner (1985) suggests that adolescence is the beginning of orientating to future circumstances. Jenny found it hard to create images of her future lifestyle and living arrangements.

During one of her occupational therapy sessions Jenny interviewed her occupational therapist using a dictaphone. The aim of the session was to explore the use of a tape recorder as a method for recording her school work and personal thoughts. Jenny asked me, as her therapist, a series of questions focusing on my experience of high school and adolescence. I felt she was perhaps building on other people's stories, comparing them to her own, while trying to create her own present story as a step toward the future. In effect, she was modelling her future on other people's experiences.

Timing was important to Jenny. She needed to determine when she carried out aspects of her therapy, for example, when she stopped using the hoist to get out of bed. She required control over the timing of when she attempted tasks and if this did not occur, she would refuse to participate.

Mattingly (1994a) suggests that story time, as in human time, is shaped by motive and intention. Sacks (1984), clinical professor of neurology and author, describes his own experience during injury to illustrate this point:

> *I looked at my watch to see if it had stopped but the second hand was going round with perfect regularity. Its time, abstract, impersonal, chronological, had no relation to my time – my time which consisted solely of personal moments, life moments, critical moments. (p. 8)*

Prospective future story – 'heading home'

A number of times, Jenny said that she did not want to return home, I felt that she couldn't see herself returning there. Some team members felt this was related to issues of relationships and bonding. Jenny and I had previously discussed her concerns about going home. This theme resurfaced during an occupational therapy session planned to look at kitchen skills. Although she had previously enjoyed cooking Jenny had been reluctant to go, as she was currently on a strict diet. She was also unsure whether she wanted to do this activity without her mother. On the planned day, Jenny became angry and refused to go. After her anger subsided, Jenny identified her feelings of anger as an expression of missing her family and the impact of her problems on them. This realisation culminated in her statement, 'I want to go home'. Figure 5.4 highlights the elements of emplotment at that stage.

Following this, the nursing staff began to organise a home visit for a special occasion. This was discussed with her parents; her mother was happy and a bit emotional, while her father expressed concern about their ability to cope.

During Jenny's therapy session, she spent time working out strategies that would enable her to discuss her worries with her parents. She was angry that she didn't have a say about when the home visit should occur, but she showed insight into why it was not an appropriate step for her at that stage. Jenny remarked at the end of that session, 'I know I want to go home, but I'm not sure if I'm ready yet'.

For the team, this presented as an area of conflict because various team members had different perspectives on the value of and reasons behind the visit. When reflecting on this particular incident, I could see there were, in fact, different stories occurring at the same time. While there were perhaps common images of the future, the views on how Jenny would get there and the steps needed varied considerably.

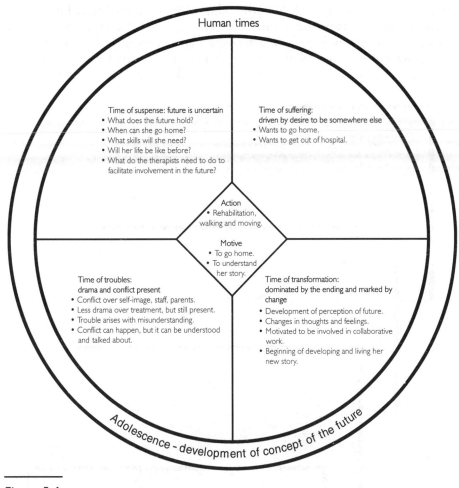

Figure 5.4

Emplotment of Jenny's future narrative: 'heading home'.

Figure 5.5 illustrates the layers of stories in use at this stage of the narrative and the concerns and perspectives of members of the rehabilitation team. Mattingly and Gillette (1991) suggest that there are times when multiple story interpretations do not blend into a single story and, instead, reflect different ways of interpreting the same clinical situation. Also, Uden *et al.* (1992) suggest that if nurses and physicians interpret their experiences within different stories, this may lead to conflict. They stress the importance of agreement on a common frame story.

Using narrative reasoning as part of my work increased my depth of understanding of communication and made me listen to the stories people tell. It is often not the story itself but the point of the story to the listener and the reason it is told that is important (Mattingly, 1994a). Following this, I felt more empowered to iron out misunderstandings before they escalated into greater difficulties. I also felt that conflict was an underlying impetus which enabled a story to move toward the future and was therefore an inevitable aspect of rehabilitation. I could then creatively use these themes to assist Jenny to develop greater understanding and greater control.

Occupational therapist/physiotherapist
Feel it is unrealistic for Jenny to go home as yet as she has not reached the physical goals required for her home environment and therefore safety would be a problem.
Needs to be structured so she and her family will succeed.
She is not ready physically or emotionally.
She needs to have a say in when it happens and be part of the planning.

Nursing staff/medical staff
Some of the nurses feel that this family has been separated for too long and that this has interfered with their relationship. They see it as positive to go home for a visit. They feel Jenny should not dictate when things happen. Other nurses are annoyed at the lack of teamwork and preparation.

Parents
Mum was really pleased and started to cry. This would be the first time getting her home. She can see her coming home in the future.
Dad was really worried about how she would cope getting into the house. Perhaps he is thinking what it will be like in the future. He is worried the hospital will think he doesn't want her to come home and doesn't feel able to talk to the staff about this.

Jenny
She really wants to go home for the day. She has been told it will be arranged. She is angry because she didn't have a say in it. She is also scared she won't cope physically, as she has not yet practised stairs in physiotherapy. She is also worried about coping with her feelings. She doesn't feel ready to do it, but feels everyone expects her to go home.
She knows she wants to.......But!

Figure 5.5

Layers of stories: the issue is going home for a visit.

THEMES OF THE NARRATIVE

The experience of narrative

This narrative was not originally told or experienced in a linear or chronological fashion. It was through my reflective processes and through writing this narrative down that it appears to have taken this form. The narrative was experienced as different layers that refolded on each other, moving in and out of the past. Each new piece of information became integrated into the story, how it might link to the past, what it meant to the present and what it could mean in the future.

It wasn't just Jenny's story but was also the story of those around her, family and those working with her. The aspects of the story interweave, making it difficult to separate them. This represents the nature of narratives and why narrative reasoning is an essential component of occupational therapy reasoning.

This narrative also elicited a number of emotions, linking them historically with critical incidents and placing them in the context of the relationship in which they occurred. In the outlined narrative, the emotions were not just Jenny's feelings of fear, hate, anger or loss of control. They were also the feelings of her parents – grief, anxiety, loss. Similarly, the feelings of the staff working with them – frustration at not making it right, guilt and sadness at the tragic nature of the young girl's story.

Impact of changes in emplotment

One of the noticeable aspects of this case story was the change of emplotment and reemplotment within the story, illustrated in Figures 5.2–5.4. The story begins with the main action centred on medical needs, with gradual changes towards a future rehabilitation story being voiced. The motives of the story also changed. All these changes in emplotment highlight how important it is to know the story and how the story is told. If the person working with Jenny or her parents was at a different stage of emplotment, this could have created misunderstandings or the feeling of being lost. There is a need to constantly revise and reframe the story (Mattingly, 1994a).

The role of conflict

In using a narrative approach, troubles are seen as a necessary part of enacting a story, being the impetus required for the spiral of emplotment to continue. In occupational therapy emplotment, the patient, or narrative hero, is in alliance with the therapist, waging a war or conflict to overcome adversity (Mattingly, 1994a,b). Conflict is therefore inherent.

Timing

If we do not understand or know a family's sense of time and do not pace the timing of our interventions, there is potential for misunderstanding. If the team does not understand a family's timing and planning of future events, it may enforce an action before the family is ready. In Jenny's story, there was a potentially conflicting situation in giving her permission to go home for the day. This shows why careful planning is required by the team to make decisions that consider the timing of and readiness for the next step.

Associated with the concept of time is the stage in the person's lifecycle. Jenny entered adolescence at the beginning of her therapeutic story and her behaviour was partly a response to this. Testing out control in decision making, deciding whether to meet parental expectations and developing an identity are all aspects of this life stage (Steinberg, 1990).

Jenny's difficulty in dealing with these aspects was perceived by some members of the team as refusal and rudeness. Zegans (1989) suggests that when a part of a patient's body escapes their control, their identity, status, competency and empowerment are questioned. It is therefore even harder to exercise choice and individuality, when a sense of this is not fully established. This was emphasised by Jenny's choice of staff to work with her and her attachment to key members of staff.

Future images

Having placed past images in a temporal context, it is important to acknowledge the existence of future images or where this person's future lies. Often this is not communicated to clients, as therapists and medical staff do not know the answers to what will ultimately happen in the future.

Difficulty is often experienced when helping families to support rehabilitation efforts and to be goal oriented, by offering hope and encouragement, while also sensitively and empathically communicating realistic and possibly negative future images (McLaughlin and Carey, 1993).

Working together: future images

Within teams, several types of reasoning occur according to differences in personal experiences, disciplinary backgrounds, organisational roles, interests and the individuals' epistemological basis of practice (Ryan, 1995). This was particularly noted in Jenny's story when the issue of going home for the day was first considered.

According to Crepeau (1994), a team, when working together, develops a shared meaning about the person and uses a common language to describe that person's story. During team meetings, goals are planned and the team collectively constructs the meaning and understanding of the patient's perspective. Staff members debate in order to identify the troubles experienced by the patient and to establish a common definition of the patient's problems. Team members are forming a unified picture, to develop an understanding of the story. In Jenny's story, the importance of developing a common story or understanding of the possible future was highlighted in the layers of stories featured in Figure 5.5. In Jenny's story this was not explicit and some of the occupational therapist's time was spent assisting others to understand her story. This was achieved by relaying the stories told by Jenny and interpreting those told to others.

A basic conflict arises within the work of some teams which centres on the relationship with the family members of the patient in therapy who often expect that there is a cure in rehabilitation (McLaughlin and Carey, 1993). When people are working together, it is therefore important that they are aware of the different images each team member holds. For instance, the family may have future images of a full recovery which could be quite different from the doctor's image.

An occupational therapist's role

Mattingly and Fleming (1994) suggest that responding to a difficult case may require the creation of an individualised role for the therapist, which can often take therapists outside preconceived role boundaries.

Peloquin (1993) searches for visions and images of relationships using ideas of technician, parent and friend. In illuminating the roles gained from the discussion, Peloquin writes, 'Recommitment to regarding the patient as a partner or friend can lead to exchanges marked by mutuality, caring and competence'. Stories of caring encourage these roles of storyteller, translator and advocate (Coles, 1989).

My role in working with Jenny changed within the narrative. I had a rehabilitation role as a member of the team by assisting her in developing skills in feeding, dressing, using a wheelchair, writing, meal preparation and time use within the hospital. I also identified other possible roles: the role of advocate in translating and interpreting her story (Lythgoe, personal communication), the varying role of storyteller or interpreter (Ryan, personal communication), and the role of friend (Medhurst, personal communication). I used Jenny's stories to explain to staff how her experiences affected her motivation and feelings towards her rehabilitation.

Storytelling and story making

The case story described used narrative reasoning to gain an understanding of the client's situation, as well as planning for her future. There were aspects of 'storytelling', linking the client with the present involvement in occupational therapy and the 'story making' of a prospective future.

This method of reasoning allows for greater reflection and the use of artistic ways of working by highlighting the nature and uniqueness of the individual's situation. With greater understanding of our client's situation, we can value and respect our clients as well as develop our recognition of mismatched story emplotments, of timing, information and language.

Conflict, then, is viewed as an active element of a narrative and it provides the energy needed to solve problems creatively. As we continue to question what story we are in, occupational therapists need also to remember, 'The patient does not come to therapy. Rather, therapy comes into the patient's life' (Helfrich and Kielhofner, 1994).

Further thoughts

1 Take a critical incident from your own life story and write it down in as much detail as possible. Talk to others involved in this incident and compare and contrast the differing stories.
2 Imagine you are 'Jenny' in this story. How might you have reacted to the situation as described? In what ways would this knowledge have helped you to identify your therapeutic intervention had you been the therapist?

3 Consider a client with whom you are currently involved or one from your fieldwork experiences. Try to imagine their unfolding therapeutic story. Illustrate these layers using the author's figures as a template.

4 Taking a case story as a focal point, interview three people who have been involved with this person, to explore their different story perspectives. What are the implications of these findings for therapy and team working?

REFERENCES

Coe, R. (1995) Layers of stories: narrative reasoning in paediatric occupational therapy. Unpublished manuscript, University of East London.

Coles, R. (1989) *The Call of Stories*. Houghton Mifflin, Boston.

Crepeau, E. B. (1994) Three images of interdisciplinary team meetings. *American Journal of Occupational Therapy*, **48**(8), 717–722.

Gans, J. S. (1983) Hate in the rehabilitation team. *Archives of Physical Medicine and Rehabilitation*, **64**, 176–179.

Helfrich, C., Kielhofner, G. (1994) Volitional narratives and the meaning of therapy. *American Journal of Occupational Therapy*, **48**(4), 319–326.

Kielhofner, G. (1985) *A Model of Human Occupation*. Williams and Wilkins, Baltimore.

Mattingly, C. (1991) Narrative reflections on practical actions: two learning experiments in reflective storytelling. In D. A. Schon, (ed.) *The Reflective Turn: Case Studies In and On Educational Practice*. Teacher's College Press, New York.

Mattingly, C. (1994a) The narrative nature of clinical reasoning. In C. Mattingly and M. H. Fleming, (eds) *Clinical Reasoning: Forms of Inquiry in a Therapeutic Practice*. F. A. Davis, Philadelphia.

Mattingly, C. (1994b) The concept of therapeutic 'emplotment'. *Social Science and Medicine*, **38**(6), 811–822.

Mattingly, C., Fleming, M. H. (1994) *Clinical Reasoning: Forms of Inquiry in a Therapeutic Practice*. F. A. Davis, Philadelphia.

Mattingly, C., Gillette, N. (1991) Anthropology, occupational therapy and action research. *American Journal of Occupational Therapy*, **45**(11), 972–978.

McLaughlin, A. M., Carey, J. L. (1993) The adversarial alliance: developing therapeutic relationships between families and the team in brain injury rehabilitation. *Brain Injury*, **7**(1), 45–51.

Medhurst, A. (1996) Clinical reasoning in local authority paediatric occupational therapy: planning a major adaptation for a child with a degenerative condition, part 2. *British Journal of Occupational Therapy*, **59**(6), 269–272.

Peloquin, S. M. (1993) The depersonalisation of patients: a profile gleaned from narratives. *American Journal of Occupational Therapy*, **47**(9), 830–837.

Ryan, S. E. (1990) Clinical reasoning: a descriptive study comparing novice and expert therapists. Unpublished Masters thesis, Columbia University, New York.

Ryan, S. E. (1995) The study and application of clinical reasoning research. *British Journal of Therapy and Rehabilitation*, **2**(5), 265–271.

Sacks, O. (1984) *A Leg to Stand On*. Pan Books, London.

Steinberg, L. (1990) *Adolescence*. McGraw-Hill, New York.

Uden, G., Norberg, A., Linseth, A., Marhaug, V. (1992) Ethical reasoning in nurses' and physicians' stories about care episodes. *Journal of Advanced Nursing*, **17**, 1028–1034.

Zegans, L. S. (1989) The body and personal integration in health and illness. In B. W. Heller, L. M. Flohr and L. S. Zegans, (eds) *Psychosocial Interventions with Physically Disabled Persons*. Jessica Kingsley, London.

6 THE TEAM'S STORY OF A CLIENT'S EXPERIENCE OF ANOREXIA NERVOSA

Ruth Erica Living

KEY POINTS
- Work philosophy
- 'Time' in treatment
- Multiple stories forming one narrative
- Changing focus of treatment at different stages

Several stories are pulled together to form the basis of this chapter. Alison's progress through treatment is told by multiple voices from key members of the treatment team. These stories illustrate that different aspects of Alison were revealed or focused on by different staff. In the overall story there was some overlapping as well as gaps in the narrative. Most importantly, Alison's voice is not heard and this could be a topic for further discussion in trying to understand the client's lifeworld through the treatment process. The story reveals the changing tones as Alison progresses, the highs and lows of her illness experience and her turning points towards health.

Alison is a 36-year-old woman whose life has been affected by the eating disorder anorexia nervosa. Her real name is not used in order to preserve her confidentiality. The story centres on Alison's last admission as an inpatient on an eating disorder unit in the south east of England. It was told to me retrospectively by the team of professionals who worked with her. I will describe the background in order to set the scene. Then various factors involving the intervention that took place will be explored in terms of critical incidents which highlight the process of change for Alison.

The work presented here came about for three reasons. First, while I was working as an occupational therapist within community mental health settings, I became involved in working with clients with anorexia nervosa. At that time I had little knowledge of this area but grew to find it both challenging and rewarding. I particularly remember one occasion when a client gave me a copy of the book by Maureen Dunbar (1986) about her daughter Catherine's struggle with, and eventual death from, anorexia nervosa. I remember this occasion vividly as the client gave me the book with the proviso that reading it wouldn't make me anorexic. In fact, reading it didn't make me anorexic but provided me with an insight into this complex experience. This fuelled a continuing dedication to understanding this process and how intervention can aid recovery.

Sometimes I see this client on the commuter train to London, the last time being a few months ago. She is always amazed that my experience of working with anorexic people hasn't made me an anorexic. She is also glad that more stories can be told to widen the general understanding of this disorder. The idea for the investigation was formed within clinical practice and was refined later, through my work on the Masters programme at the University of East London.

The second reason for choosing this area of investigation is the apparent rise in the number of people, mostly women and often adolescents, seeking help for their condition. I see this as a possible growth area for occupational therapy involvement. According to the Eating Disorders Association, the demand for support for sufferers, their family and friends is reflected in their statistics. Anorexia nervosa has the potential to affect a large group of people.

Finally, the third reason focuses on food as a central aspect of life necessary for survival and health. In Western society it is interesting that many people can enjoy food without it becoming an issue, whilst for others it can become a way of expressing emotions and lack of self-worth.

This chapter will focus on Alison's experience of anorexia nervosa. It is important to state that the client's story is told solely by the professional team and that Alison herself was not asked to contribute at any point. It presents a composite story from the team, selected from a wider investigation which explored the use of narratives.

BACKGROUND

The storytellers for this enquiry were five members of a multidisciplinary team on an in-patient unit for people with eating disorder in the south of England. Those contributing their stories were the consultant psychiatrist, occupational therapist, nurse specialist, dietician and music therapist. It has long been recognised that people with mental health problems such as eating disorders require an organised and well-coordinated team of professionals to ensure that their needs are met in a holistic way. Ryan (1995) stressed the uniqueness of each team member in terms of their experience, organisational role, interest and epistemological basis of practice. It is recognised that each health-care professional must attempt to work effectively within the team, including the client, to achieve a shared meaning of the client's story. The multidisciplinary team at the centre of this narrative had a wealth of experience in this field. Meetings held weekly offered the opportunity for these team members to share their stories of the clients at the unit.

In terms of the unit's overall philosophy, this narrative provided an insight into how it is enacted in practice. The six factors shown below were identified by the team as underpinning their chosen way of working.

1 On admission, patients were required to restrict their activity levels.
2 The amount of food consumed was increased by the client. No reward system existed.
3 No target weight was set at admission but rather as progress was made. According to the consultant, 'To talk about the kind of weights one's looking

for . . . the 50 kilograms seems an unachievable target to them and the length of time, if they bother to work out a standard rate of gain per week, would look as if they were going to be in hospital forever'.

4 Changes to the patient's programme, such as the nature and number of groups and readiness for weekend leave, were made at the weekly team meeting. Patients could submit written requests to the team for consideration. Decisions were reviewed and alterations set as a team to ensure continuity and to avoid the possibility of manipulation by clients.

5 Clients needed to gain weight before attending groups which were held outside the unit.

6 Weight gain was associated with psychological insight. As illustrated by the consultant's story, 'An ability to eat independently, to plan meals, to have time at home and for that to have gone satisfactorily . . . that patients are able to renegotiate some of their relationships at home . . . so that they don't just go back to what they came from'.

Because of the client's low body weight and the intense struggle for autonomy, the need for intervention at this stage addressed the client's total needs. The prevention of further deterioration was vital. The client's experience can therefore be intense. This meant that if the intervention was to have meaning, the health-care professionals needed to ensure that they had a shared concept of the client's story. Working within such a dynamic framework inevitably created its own pressures which sometimes made this process difficult. Narrative could be easily lost within procedures such as 'refeeding', which might lead to a focus on weight gain only. The reader will find that the story to be told does not exhibit this, due to the overall team philosophy, their chosen ways of working and their close communication. The client, as a person, was placed at the centre of the intervention.

ALISON

Alison was born in London, England, in the winter of 1963 following a 'normal birth', a sibling for her older sister. Early in life she was hospitalised for a bowel infection but otherwise was physically healthy throughout childhood. Her childhood years are described as happy, although she was the victim of bullying during her primary and secondary schooling. This no doubt led to some degree of emotional upset for her. Adolescence was then characterised by further anxiety as she worried about examinations but nevertheless went on to pass three Advanced Level examinations. Alison's family life was seemingly very insular and self-contained in that:

The parents didn't have many friends, they weren't out all the time, they didn't socialise much, they were very much a contained family without a lot of extended family. So family events were small, they didn't entertain very much. There weren't many people who came back in to the house, the family home. (The occupational therapist's story)

Alison took on the role of helper at home for her parents and had little opportunity to satisfy her own needs. The reason for this, beyond the enmeshed nature of the family, is not clear.

Following the school years Alison's early adulthood was marked by leaving home for further study in the field of catering. She later progressed to study management. Alison recognised that she found it very difficult to be with her peers in a student environment This was perhaps because of her previously limited social contacts. In 1988 her first admission with anorexia nervosa occurred; she was an inpatient for three months. Little is known of this admission other than that Alison gained weight.

In 1989, Alison's father underwent major surgery and died shortly afterwards in 1990, aged 60. It is not known how much of an impact this had on Alison at the time, given her early closeness with her family and continued closeness with her mother. During this period Alison was once more an inpatient for anorexia nervosa, again for three months. This same year Alison returned to a learning situation and retrained in accountancy.

She appeared to live a very narrow existence revolving around work that she did not actually like but which she felt offered a sense of security and familiarity. However, it did become the source of a fear of rejection. She was concerned that 'they [the employer] will say she is not needed any more' which, as events proceeded, proved to be a well-founded fear. It was at that point that Alison's use of activity to avoid eating became evident. As a result her weight loss began. She did not make time to eat when at work, failing to stop for food at lunch time because she wanted to:

> . . . *make sure that her work was all up to date and nobody could say Alison's work was shoddy or whatever. The difficulty for Alison was in terms of when she was going to have lunch and how long it was going to take. (The nurse's story)*

Alison's particular tasks at work were separate from the rest of her colleagues and despite attempts to make her more part of the team, Alison managed to work alone as she did not like working with others. She preferred instead to have 'her own bit' as 'If you have your own bit you can control it, otherwise who knows what will happen?'. Alison presents as someone who is 'quite self-assured, quite forthright in her views, rather rigid, with some obsessive traits'. She *'likes to be thinking all the time [and] to be doing, which is evident in her work pattern'* (The consultant's story).

Alison's life at this time was described as being 'empty of significant others'. Her social life was restricted to people from her workplace who were 'more like acquaintances than friends'. She did not have many emotional commitments and no current sexual relationship, no children and she lived alone. She had regular contact with her mother who lived, and continues to live, nearby. She had very irregular contact with her sister, now a single parent, who lived some distance away. As well as a physical distance between the sisters there also appeared to be an emotional one which was again not accounted for.

Alison did, however, have a range of hobbies including dough making for which she had attended courses. She also liked exercise, especially badminton, but not obsessively. She played a key role in amateur dramatics, organising backstage rather than acting. Alison also went to a singles' club. These hobbies were to play a significant role in her life later on.

Alison's adulthood was characterised by two further hospital admissions in 1993 and this current one beginning in February 1997. In general, little is known about previous admissions except that Alison always gained weight rather rapidly and consequently experienced very painful physical side-effects.

THE REFERRAL

Alison was physically debilitated, not eating or drinking properly. So when she was referred for this current admission as an extra contractual referral by the psychiatric services where she had been seen by a nurse counsellor for a 'few months but it wasn't having any effect on her', she was a very low weight at 29 kg. Despite her poor physical state, Alison continued to work right up to the day that she came for assessment. At this stage, Alison was eating three small meals daily, at very strict times. Small portions were a habit and she was literally afraid to eat too much. Her meals consisted of extremely small portions of cereal and toast; morning coffee; sandwiches with stewed fruit and yoghurt; afternoon tea; evening meal of chicken; milky drink with biscuits. Mealtimes were accompanied by rituals concerning food preparation and the placement of plates and utensils. Feelings of fullness and bloatedness always prevented her from eating more. However, she never used laxatives or diet pills to aid weight loss and never induced vomiting. She rarely looked at herself in the mirror and would only weigh herself at her GP's surgery.

THE ADMISSION

Alison was admitted in February 1997. At this time clients with eating disorders were treated on an acute admissions ward. Some staff were away on annual leave and this caused considerable upset for Alison who felt that nothing was right about the unit. She expressed a wish to go home. The occupational therapist's story conveys Alison's initial sense of a lack of hope, that this admission was going to be no different from the previous ones. This is expressed clearly in terms of Alison's expectations that 'I've been there, done that, got the T-shirt' and a sense of 'scrapping' going on between Alison and the team. The central plot focuses upon Alison's reaction to the programme with accounts of her anger, frustration and identification of the change process. This was a gradual process in which the need for completion and repetition is voiced. Part of this involved Alison checking out the boundaries and identifying the shared level of trust with the team. The occupational therapist expressed how such behaviour provided insights into Alison's experience:

> *It was about her feeling that we were accepting and we were going to accept her and stay with it. Then she began to feel safe and when she did put weight on, she started to look at issues which distressed her.*

The consultant's story of Alison's behaviour at this time voiced similar issues. He said:

> Unless she engineered you into saying things like, you've got to go, we couldn't care less, there's nothing we can do for you, she actually stuck with the treatment. So we had to put up with that behaviour at the beginning.

Initially, life on the unit was characterised by a period of enforced inactivity, so ensuring that Alison had the full benefits of nutrition. From the nurse's story:

> She found it very difficult in quiet spaces, she feels she's lazy. She kept saying how bored she was and asked the staff 'How can you do this to me?' Nothing was basically right. If the ward routine was disturbed or altered in any way she became very upset and exhibited 'lots of controlling, obsessional type behaviour'.

At the point of admission Alison was considerably thinner than many of the others on the unit but recognised she was atypical in that she had an unusual level of insight into her condition. It was evident that she realised she was thin but she did not have a distorted body image. Her eating pattern meant that Alison experienced a range of physical complaints including endocrine and nasogastric problems. She also had amenorrhoea as a consequence of her low weight and felt herself to be ugly due to hair on her face and arms, about which she was very self-conscious. She was very tense and wanted to be busy and 'more like the hare than the tortoise' (the occupational therapist's story). It was therefore especially important for Alison to slow down, to allow her body to take advantage of the nutrition she was now receiving but, also, to strengthen her emotionally for the work that she was to do.

THE EARLY DAYS ON THE UNIT

It was the nurse's story that provided most insight into Alison's life at this time in terms of the way in which she coped whilst she was on the ward. It provided understanding into her reaction to not being allowed to participate in activity, as well as her problems communicating with her fellow patients. The nurse's story provided many examples of the nurse being in tune with Alison's anxieties. For example, on admission:

> I guess coming into a new place there are lots of anxieties going on within you and around you not knowing people.

Much was said concerning the initial period of rest when Alison was not able to leave the unit, her angry response to this, her continual pushing for more to do and for weekend leave. The lack of a reward system was indicated as being important and that all clients were able to go at their own pace. On previous admissions it was noted that Alison ate to gain weight in order to 'get out'. But on this unit her weight gain was slower which provided an opportunity for her to gain a sense of acceptance of her physical and emotional changes. At this stage, consistency in the team approach was deemed important and self-support amongst the clients was encouraged. It was the nurse's story that identified that the move to the purpose-built unit was having a beneficial impact on Alison and other patients, as the environment was centred on their needs. She recalled an incident that occurred whilst on the acute unit. Alison was confronted by another patient who did not have an eating disorder, who 'pulled her blouse at the top and said, "I've always wanted to see a bag of bones" and Alison took that quite well'. She responded, 'Now I know who my friends are' rather than becoming upset and withdrawing to her room. Tensions between clients with different mental health needs were a possible source of difficulty, hence the move to the purpose-built unit.

Alison was described by this nurse as 'a very guarded person. You couldn't get too much below the skin'. This reserve prevented the team from identifying possible triggers for her condition. It also impacted on her relationships with other clients. Initially, she often kept herself physically outside the social circle of fellow patients, although she would often sit near to the group, seemingly waiting and wanting to be drawn in:

> When they were chatting out there [indicating a lounge area] if they did include her she'd be sitting there but sitting aside from them, if they drew her into the conversation she would take part but she wouldn't come out as some people do . . . she would be there but not be there. (The nurse's story)

Following angry outbursts on the ward, Alison was known to apologise although at times this was difficult for her to do. The nursing perspective on these outbursts was that, 'She was just trying to cope with what's going on around her. It was just bad luck for whoever went in there with her'; her anger was not aimed at anyone personally. It therefore seemed that Alison found it very difficult to relate to other people on the unit at this stage. The occupational therapist spoke of Alison as having a physical emptiness in terms of not eating as well as an emotional void due to the absence of others in her life. Her relationship with her mother remained constant and she visited regularly. Alison did, however, get upset at times when she and her mother had minor arguments, 'like all people do'.

Whilst on the unit, Alison also wanted to make sure that she did not eat large portions because on previous admissions when her weight gain had been rapid, it had been accompanied by very painful oedema and bloatedness which she was now anxious to avoid. She also wanted to retain the possibility of feeling hungry at each meal which could be achieved by keeping portions small. The dietician reported that Alison used her knowledge of food, gained from her catering background, to good advantage in terms of planning her menus and supporting others in their treatment.

Alison also stood out as being different in terms of her maturity.

> She was less immature than many of the others; she didn't play games. She was less evasive or deceitful. She was more 'up front' about her complaints and

criticisms and viewed the other patients as being immature. She felt they wasted their in-patient time, she saw the validity of what we were doing, and she gained weight consistently. (The consultant's story)

Previous experience of in-patient admissions undoubtedly set the scene for Alison. Previous admissions had been disastrous and she had a very negative feeling about them. The occupational therapist voiced Alison's concerns in this respect:

. . . she came in with the expectation or without any expectation really, what are you going to do that is going to make any difference to my treatment? Every form of treatment that was offered was, like, well, I've done that, it didn't work then so why should this time be different?

The message the team was getting at this time was that Alison did not want to be on the unit; 'She wanted to get out and back to work as soon as possible'. She exhibited lots of resistance and often spoke of wanting to discharge herself. This proved to be an ongoing issue in her story. Despite many proclamations throughout the admission that Alison would leave, she never went against medical advice. She stayed until both she and the team believed she was ready for discharge and at a safe body weight.

Her feelings about the unit were negative for quite some time and she was at times very vocal in expressing this. Her dissatisfaction with the hospital food system was addressed by arranging to see the catering manager. This resulted in a change in the meal system which the dietician recognised was better for all the clients on the unit.

BUILDING LEVELS OF ACTIVITY

Once Alison started regaining weight, she attended groups outside the unit. The occupational therapist likened Alison's story to a 'road' which needed to be travelled and which would continue to take a different route through admission and following discharge. The road chosen involved 'much more of a cognitive model' and working in the 'here and now' rather than 'doing lots of indepth psychotherapy type work'.

This story considers the programme which was provided for Alison, how she gained insight into her progress and how she came to appreciate the decisions related to her programme made weekly by the whole team. This largely negated the possibility of manipulation by any client. The occupational therapist observed that it was Dr X who was given a 'hard time' because of some of the decisions.

As I built the story, it was difficult to pinpoint exactly how Alison's programme developed chronologically. It was evident that it included a gradual progression of activity through participation in individual and groupwork, mostly off the unit itself. At each point of the programme, Alison wanted new activities included to feed her desire to keep busy. This was monitored by staff. Alison participated in the following groups: art/pottery; music therapy; social skills; stress management; diary group; nutrition and education group. Alison used the non-verbal aspects of intervention well and communicated much more effectively in that way. Several incidents occurred in the group setting which related to Alison's ability to work in this way. On one occasion she spoke of her intense personal feeling that everything always stays the same. When challenged about this, she recognised that changes were being made but that 'It doesn't feel like it' and she acknowledged the possibility that things could change after all.

EXPRESSION OF FEELINGS

The music therapist spoke of Alison's enforced period of inactivity early on and that this was one way for the team to communicate that 'We're taking your weight seriously even though you [Alison] think it's OK'. Alison's initial scepticism that this admission was going to be any different was highlighted and the feeling of 'defeat' that any weight gain would not last. The music therapist considered that weight gain was needed before she could attend the music group.

Group participation proved to be a mixed experience for Alison, who stated that she contributed to the sessions because it was 'only polite' and that it was not very nice for the therapist if nobody said anything. This polite side of her was not evident in another session when she said, speaking for the whole group, 'No-one likes coming here – it's not about us, it's about you'. She became quite angry. This anger was expressed in a further incident when she stopped everyone from leaving the group room whilst she turned the 'Do not disturb' sign around, indicating that the room and the therapist could now be disturbed.

It was the music therapist who highlighted Alison's role in these groups. Her character in this story was presented as a very active person who used her energy to avoid 'exploring her psychological world'. Part of the change process involved her 'literally slowing down' so she could work on this aspect. The consultant provided an insight into the team's thinking about Alison's difficulty in this area:

> Our feeling, of course, is that she probably has quite major turmoil if she does look closely into her own feelings and is very fearful of being depressed and overwhelmed by all her feelings, so that's a lot of the work that's being explored now.

Also evident in groups was Alison's inability to be with the others; in sessions she would sit at a physical distance from them. She often stated that she felt older than the other patients, whom she referred to as 'the girls', and therefore that she felt isolated in some way from them. However, Alison found art a useful communication medium. She enjoyed being creative, which was evident in a mural collage that she created with other patients in their own time. Alison's design was described as being 'like jagged lightening strikes' which seemed to some of the team to be in keeping with the prickly outward persona she was projecting at that time.

The music therapist provided an image of Alison in terms of her appearance and identified several key incidents that contributed to understanding the change process that took place. Her story incorporated incidents involving anger, calmness and very human pictures of an individual's suffering presented in a creative, visual way with heavy use of metaphor. Alison's initial 'busyness' was exhibited in her music playing, her lack of confidence and self-esteem reflected in her saying 'I can't play the instruments'. Initially, she was difficult in the group and it was the music therapist who recalled the episodes of her 'not wanting to be there' and only saying things to be polite. Later in the admission, it was identified that during the groups there were moments when a 'lighter, brighter, attractive side of Alison' became evident and 'She would do something rather lovely. There was sort of holding on to this sense that she could be lovely as well'. The story projected the image that Alison 'was asked to grow, to be a person, physically and emotionally in this empty space'. This sense of growth was echoed later when speaking of the changes that Alison was able to make as being akin to a flower.

> *It was like she was blossoming almost – letting the person come out and this sort of child that never was a child somehow, you felt had never been an adult.*

The music therapist identified that she always thought of Alison as being older than she actually was and:

> *. . . that there is a sense that she was always a little old . . . and allowing her to become a young woman again.*

Change was a prominent feature of each incident and initially Alison was difficult to get close to. Again, it was the music therapist who referred to that mural which Alison had decorated: 'as intervention progressed, she became more smooth edged'.

WEIGHT GAIN AND LOSS

Alison's response to the programme created an interesting situation for her. She undoubtedly carried with her the experience from her previous admissions in which weight gain was rapid and resulted in unpleasant side-effects. On this admission, having more control over her food intake was therefore appreciated and she became very independent in meal selection and included her own sauces and fruits that she brought from home. Weight gain was slow but, most importantly, it was consistent although at times Alison found this very frustrating. The medical notes reported that she gained 8 kg over three months and at that stage weighed 37.4 kg. Alison wanted to achieve a weight of 44.5 kg but the team's goal was thought at that time to be nearer 50 kg.

Due to the slowness of her weight gain, the team delayed giving Alison weekend leave for a long time despite frequent requests from her. The consultant stated: 'Whatever team decisions we come to have been reached on the basis of deciding things very carefully'. In terms of weekend leave and Alison's anger at not being granted it earlier, the consultant acknowledged that he bore 'the brunt of her discontentment' but that it was 'within reasonable bounds'. He spoke about it objectively.

She felt at times we exploited the fact that she would . . . never discharge herself against medical advice. And she said 'You know that therefore you are able to put limits on me that I don't agree with. That you couldn't put on other people'.

As predicted, once leave was granted, Alison always lost weight over the weekend period. However, a positive outcome of this was that Alison took personal responsibility for recovering the weight lost after leave. She did not need encouragement to do so. Weekend leave was also affected as Alison's mother was away visiting a sick relative. This meant that Alison could not always go home. However, it was some time before the team would also grant midweek leave in order to prevent a dip in her weight.

As she began to gain weight and feel more in control, Alison took more interest in her appearance and put on make-up. When anyone commented on this, Alison was pleased. Her relationships with staff became less adversarial and she was generally much calmer and less defensive.

FACING DISCHARGE

During this admission the team and patients moved to a separate unit which Alison found difficult to accept and appreciate as she felt that she was unworthy of being treated in more luxurious surroundings. She wanted to be discharged before the move but this was not possible as she had not yet reached the team's target weight.

Alison's discharge always loomed. Throughout her stay Alison was continually pushing the team for a discharge date and was very anxious to return to work. However, when the discharge date arrived she presented as being 'a bit uneasy about leaving'. She had spent quite a lot of time away from the unit anyway so it was expected that she would make a 'fairly easy transition' to being a day patient. However, in a group shortly before discharge, Alison was speaking with a client who was already a day patient and who said that being discharged was not as good as everyone thought it was going to be. Alison's reaction to this was that 'I know it's not going to be great . . . I'm not silly, I've done weekends'. She exhibited an excitement about leaving and stated that 'It's time I got on with my life'. At this point Alison also expressed concern that the change and resumption of her responsibilities may be too much for her.

Prior to discharge, Alison experienced high degrees of stress as it became evident that her employers were being less than supportive, suggesting that Alison's job was under threat. As work had been identified as being the priority and structure in Alison's life and one which provided her with a sense of stability and responsibility, this created problems for her. Initially, this led to weight loss but then her newly found ability to cope came to the fore.

AFTER DISCHARGE

The story of life after discharge involved returning to a work situation that was insecure and where work had been left to pile up for the seven months she had been away. This would have been a difficult task for anyone but was particularly so for someone like Alison, who found it easy to push food to one side in order to complete her work tasks. This situation would therefore test all the progress she had made on the unit. Instead of resorting to food restrictions, Alison began to talk about herself and to express her feelings. One major step forward was explained within an art-based group in which Alison drew a picture 'with all these books on her head as a representation of all the pressure that she'd felt from various people throughout her life'. It therefore seemed that for Alison she could only address the emotional distress in her life outside the unit and after she had gained weight. Changes therefore became evident as she continued to gain weight despite her work difficulties.

Alison's story took another major turn following discharge and her once bleak future suddenly offered many changes. Alison had responded to the opportunities that presented themselves in the face of an underlying feeling that it could all disintegrate. She was now becoming more assertive at work and enjoying her crucial backstage role at the amateur dramatics group. She also began seeing a male friend from the singles' club.

PULLING IT TOGETHER

The thread which runs through the story of Alison is that of anorexia nervosa but with this last admission it was possible to see other threads emerging related to the change process. Issues related to not believing that this admission would be any different from previous ones, the expression of anger at the restrictions of the inpatient programme and continual threats to discharge herself and requests for leave recur many times.

The team's story clearly and repeatedly identified the turning points in Alison's story which were: the need for a longer admission, to gain weight slowly and build relationships which could provide the opportunity to uncover and face issues that had not surfaced before. The team identified the key to this admission as being 'time'. Each team member highlighted this to be important, especially in terms of Alison actually 'sticking with it' and completing therapy rather than gaining weight quickly and leaving halfway through any planned intervention. Completion was therefore an important issue. Three team members – the occupational therapist, nurse and consultant – clearly pinpointed the source of change for Alison as 'taking the time' that she needed to gain weight slowly and consistently, so that she could begin to uncover and explore personal issues.

The occupational therapist spoke of the team using a cognitive model and working on the 'here and now' rather than 'doing lots of in-depth psychotherapy type work' which could occur later when she was a day patient. Another key issue was difficulty relating to the boundaries placed on her by the team. Both the occupational therapist and the consultant stories echoed each other in terms of perceiving that Alison's initial negativity and anger were aimed at pushing the team to identify how far she could do that and still be accepted. Both team members identified this as the base from which to explore difficult and painful issues. It was also possible to see an overlap in the stories of the occupational therapist and music therapist in terms of

Alison's physical and emotional emptiness and lack of close relationships leading to a poorer quality of life than she needed.

THE TEAM'S REFLECTIONS ON THE OUTCOME

During the initial storytelling process, the occupational therapist's idea of how Alison's story would progress was a very narrow one. It did not include any sense of joy or real quality of life for her. Alison's future seemed to include work, hopefully without missing meals and continuing with therapy. If these three things occurred then the occupational therapist expressed her opinion that Alison 'will allow more people into her life than she has done and will begin to feel more fulfilled in a different way and won't need to be empty'. These themes were repeated by most of the team.

Once the story changed from this rather narrow one into a more fulfilling and dynamic one, the occupational therapist expressed her joy at the changes that Alison made and how far these were from the previous narrow conception of the story. The consultant described Alison as becoming the model client because of her positive outcome. The team certainly seemed to feel a real sense of achievement.

THE AUTHOR'S REFLECTION ON THE OUTCOME

At the outset it was very difficult to imagine how the story I was told by several people would come together and what the outcome could be. I was acutely aware that there were inevitably still many gaps but hoped that I had captured the flavour of the main events. It was difficult to determine how and why the outcome arose. The possible reasons have been highlighted and are for the reader to consider. For me, it was rewarding to provide a narrative account of Alison who initially had a constrained future which suddenly opened into a positive outlook. I can only trust that the progress continues and Alison has the future that she has fought for with the support of her skilled team.

Further thoughts

1 Think of a person with whom you are working. Consider the story you have formed. Write the story of this person in as much detail as possible and highlight the main areas that you feel are important.
2 Ask a member of your team to do the above exercise. Then share your stories, looking for any similarities or differences in your understandings. What might the implications be for practice?
3 This team seemed to share a similar philosophy in their approach. What are the advantages and disadvantages of working in this way?
4 Why is 'time' or the 'right time' for client change important to effective therapy?

REFERENCES

Dunbar, M. (1986) *Catherine. A Tragic Life*. Penguin Books, Harmondsworth.

Ryan, S. (1995) Teaching clinical reasoning to occupational therapists during fieldwork education. In J. Higgs and M. Jones (eds) *Clinical Reasoning in the Health Professions*. Butterworth Heinemann, Oxford.

7

A SUPPORT GROUP FOR HEAD-INJURED INDIVIDUALS: STORIES FROM THE PEER LEADER AND FACILITATOR

Alice Lowenstein and Sharan L. Schwartzberg

KEY POINTS
- Life after trauma
- Alternative ways of working
- Partnerships: learning from each other
- Spirituality

The following narratives present two people's stories of joint working outwith the accepted occupational therapy arena. These are rich accounts, told over time, of one woman, Alice, her recovery and her wish to help others in the same situation. She sought out a facilitator for the group she founded, one who would validate the group members' experiences. Sharan became this person. Sharan's story highlights creative ways of opening the group to students for developing understanding by, learning with and learning from these individuals with a head injury. Consistency of involvement for a period of time is emphasised as being significant to all involved.

My Vision of VALT
We cannot go forward without us naming our fears.
We cannot go forward without us really sharing our dreams – our hopes – our fears together.
We cannot go forward without us helping each other realise our dreams and our deepest hopes.
We cannot go forward without us asking before we do anything if it is exactly what God is asking of us.
We cannot go forward without us both in private and together asking God to help us create our dreams.
The danger is in going too fast. We have enough time.

Alice Lowenstein
September 24 1997
Brookline, Massachusetts, USA

INTRODUCTION

The editors asked me to explain my reasoning and thinking about my practice as facilitator of a peer support group for individuals with a head injury. I in turn invited Alice Lowenstein to co-author the chapter because my role was both defined by and evolved from our relationship as co-facilitators. As she originally defined it:

> *This group will be a source for teaching each of us what we need to do for our-selves so that we can live a balanced, fulfilled life, full of work that comes from us and is effective, in a community of those who listen and share stories of learn-ing life's lessons.*

Alice and I began the group in 1989. At that time I was 40 years old and Alice 52. At the time of her injury she was 48. Now I am 48, Alice is 60. We had both grown up in the same neighbourhood in Brooklyn, New York. We met in Boston when Alice was lecturing in my department. The connection was an easy one. Based upon her occupational therapist's recommendation, Alice invited me to co-facilitate the sup-port group she was forming for the new organisation, VALT, Vital Active Life after Trauma. I came to my role with knowledge of occupational therapy groupwork. Alice came to our work with her need to know what other people experienced from their injuries so she could know what the common themes of head injuries are, the common themes of all injuries, as well as how her head injury compared with other people's injuries; her life experience as a community activist who organised groups to solve problems, a mother, wife and poet.

Sharan L. Schwartzberg,
December 27 1997
Newton, Massachusetts, USA

ALICE'S STORY – THE PEER LEADER'S PERSPECTIVE

I am a 60-year-old Jewish woman. I was married to a world-famous doctor, putting his needs first so I could help him care for people in tremendous need. I dedicated my life to being a good medical wife and a good mother. Not only was I fulfilling my upbringing, girls could help but boys could be the doctors, but I was giving to the world through him. Love and truth about what was real was in the medical system. Then in 1986 when I was 48 years old, I had a severe car accident. With a cracked skull, damaged frontal lobe, flail chest, large subdural haematoma and broken arm, I was given a 1% chance of living.

I am alive because a volunteer gave me emergency medical assistance. If I had not gotten oxygen within the first five minutes, much of my brain would have died. I would not have been able to heal the way I have. If the accident had occurred in the bend in the road, I would be dead. The next county did not have anyone volunteer-ing to give emergency medical assistance. I am alive because of the kindness and dedication of strangers, Christian strangers. My understanding of the history of the

Jews, virulent anti-Semitism which was at its height under Hitler, my shame at being a Jew, did not allow me to integrate my debt for my life to a Christian stranger.

I chose to live. I knew life was about learning to be loving and more compassionate. Filled with God's love, my soul came back to a body who thought there was no God. My reality could not be explained by my mind's map of the world. My body spoke in symptoms. I was naked. Strangers touched all parts of me. I depended upon them for my life. All the strangers wore special clothes so you could tell what rank they had. Everyone could see all of me, because I kept kicking the covers trying to get out of this nightmare. It was as if I was the only one on a nude beach. Everyone else was dressed, watching me be ashamed and humiliated.

There were no words. My thoughts moved like blocks to make sentences. Without words, I knew what everyone thought and felt. It was quite confusing to have someone smile at me, when I knew they were enraged. The most surprising part of coming back was watching how everyone denied it was love they were searching for. Everyone was looking for love. The doctors were the most loved. I could tell how loved from the changes in nurses' voices when a doctor was around.

My soul was learning how to connect to my body. I would want to do something but it hadn't learned how to tell the body. Nobody told me I would have to learn how to read this body, how to get it to do what I want it to do. The most confusing part was how people said I had to relearn everything, but then never acknowledged that I had to relearn toilet training, how the note behind my bed said I was allergic to milk, but the food was made with milk. I came into a world where what the doctor said was true. Nobody except my psychiatrist asked me what I experienced or how I was different from the way I was before.

It was so dangerous to speak about what I experienced, even if I could have found the words I forgot. I thought I had broken a taboo because nobody was speaking about where I'd been. The way children learn what is taboo is because nobody speaks about it. Even when my psychiatrist asked me to speak to the medical students about my experience or my home OT asked me to speak to her class, I was not able to speak about my whole experience. My healing has been a process of putting into words, into poems, into letters to doctors, into a diary, so that the next day I can access more of the experience.

Without body work, without someone sharing with me what my body was feeling, I could never have recaptured all of my experience. Without knowing that so many people would be helped, I would never have been able to override the protective memory loss. For those who treat head-injured people to know what they experience, they have to ask them. Ask the patient to tell you. To tell you later when they are able to name it. When a person is in the middle of anything, they cannot find words to describe it. It is only after it has been integrated, after it has been processed, that all the words come.

Three years after the accident, I was drinking coffee in the teachers' lounge at the Boston School of Occupational Therapy at Tufts University. The support group I had been in had just fired our facilitator. The better we got, the more she charged. She was never going to let us become like her. She was too attached to knowing more than we did, the way a mother knows more than her young children. I was so proud of us head-injured people talking among ourselves and firing her that I told Professor Schwartzberg about it. The group had commissioned me to find a new facilitator.

I was creating a new organisation which would discover what the head-injured patient's experience actually was. Sharan came for an interview. She was talking to me about how she would be paid. I told her about my vision for VALT. She offered to work for us for free in exchange for being able to do research as well as using the group to teach her students. None of us had read or had described to us how anyone else experienced a head injury. I knew that as I could describe it in a poem, then the group would speak about how this was alike or different for them. Without us having some description, none of us can begin. We are burdened by what others observe from the outside as describing our experience.

The difficulties we were having are no different from the people of South Africa reading books about England which do not describe their reality. Or the difficulties women have when society takes the man's experience as everyone's. The themes of experience are universal. The details are not.

SHARAN'S STORY – THE OCCUPATIONAL THERAPIST FACILITATOR'S PERSPECTIVE

As I recall, Alice interviewed me in December of 1989. The group began meeting in February of 1990. Today, September 10 1997, Alice and I met to recall the beginning of our relationship and the formation and development of the group. We sat and talked in Alice's lovely house surrounded by her beautiful gardens. It was here in Alice's living room that we seriously talked of my involvement as facilitator of a support group she was forming. We had met briefly at my school when Alice came as a guest lecturer to talk of her experience of being head-injured.

I wanted to work with the group because it would bring me into the world of people with disability. Although I had no experience of working with people with a head injury, I was confident in my group leadership skills and felt an immediate attachment for Alice. You see, she too was Jewish, transplanted from New York to Boston, and had sons. I would not accept payment for my work. I wanted to be free to write about the group and learn from the participants. To accomplish this aim, I could not struggle with billing and collecting money from participants or third-party payers. I believed reciprocity was more in keeping with the partnership model of a peer-led group. It would also discourage the formation of a hierarchical relationship with the group, as occurs in a therapist-dominated group.

Group participants were all members of a peer-developed support group formed by Alice, the director of VALT (Vital Active Life after Trauma, Inc.), a non-profit organisation. The mission of this organisation was to create support systems for head-injured survivors, their families and caregivers. One of the aims of VALT was to educate health-care professionals through the process of having head-injured survivors tell the stories of their experiences.

The group was composed of about 13 members, mostly women. There was usually a core group of 4–6 people at every meeting. The group had an open membership. In addition to seeing each other in the group, members also spoke on the phone and socialised in each other's homes and in a variety of settings such museums, theatres and restaurants. All informants lived independently in single-family dwellings or apartments, either alone, with family members or roommates. Members were approximately 35–50 years of age, college educated and had suffered a traumatic head injury. Some members worked as paid employees, volunteers or freelance workers or were students, mostly on a part-time basis. Other participants were not formally employed or had major responsibilities of caring for a home and children. Meetings took place in Alice's comfortable and elegant home in a suburb of greater Boston, Massachusetts. The members joined the group upon Alice's recommendation and my agreement. Referrals were made by word of mouth as the group and organisation became informally and later more formally recognised.

I was very unclear about my role as group facilitator and an occupational therapist. What was this? Was it therapy? Occupational therapy? Was the group different as a support group versus a therapy group? What were the boundaries to my role? These questions pressed on me and my sense of duty as a professional. The answers evolved with the group's involvement, development and process. My role also shifted, as did the group's process as needs changed.

In February 1992 Alice wrote to me:

> You said yesterday you didn't know what your role was or how this group was effective. This is very clear to me, to Debby, even to Diana who was only here once. You represent the NORMAL WORLD, you also represent the training of caregivers. THE FACT THAT YOU ARE INTERESTED IN WHAT WE SAY, YOU ARE INTERESTED AND WANT TO UNDERSTAND WHAT HAPPENED, HOW WE WERE TREATED, WHAT WE EXPERIENCED NO MATTER HOW AWFUL, IS A VERY POSITIVE FORCE FOR HEALING IN THE GROUP.
>
> Your presence, your interest, your continued wonder in asking, your insistence that you need to be explained to, you not taking the EXPERT ROLE TELLING US EVERYTHING, KNOWING AND NOT LISTENING, leads us to believe what VALT is doing actually can be done. Without VALT, without all the others on the Board, the National Advisors, the group would not be as powerful. You represent all the forces for learning, the forces for healing in the world. My role as having healed in a world which works, in having a world-famous psychiatrist who listened, who didn't know but asked, who says he is learning from me as we create new ways for treatment, my also having organised all these people to learn from us, is also powerful. However, without you, without the caring, without the interest in us as people, as thinking people, my role would be speaking in isolation. Nobody believes without having the experiences.
>
> Everyone who comes to the group is shown what I have experienced by you. The way people learn is by experience. Just the way your students give you credibility now that I spoke to them, this is the same thing you give us. Actually in our society, credibility is the prime issue for all of us. Many times we feel powerless,

the person knows so much, they are in power, we are in need even related to tech-
nical things, that we don't speak up.
Peace and Love, Alice

As Alice validated, group participants were the primary informants that guided my role as group leader. In the first year or so of the group, Alice and I had weekly phone conferences to talk about the group's process and our reactions and to plan the next meeting's agenda. The theoretical basis of my actions came from both my knowledge of occupational therapy group work and exposure to principles of humanistic psychology. Hilary Bender, my earlier primary mentor in the latter phenomenological clinical approach, was coincidentally Alice's therapist. My colleague Maureen Neistadt, one of Alice's former occupational therapists and an expert in cognitive and perceptual problems, helped me to understand head injury. In order to function in the group, I relied a great deal on what Maureen told me about the relationship between what I saw and what was invisible in the brain itself. The discussions about neurological aetiology and related occupational functioning guided my interactions. Alice commented recently that both she and I were helped in order to even function in this group. She explained:

'I was helped by Dr Jo Solet, my second home occupational therapist, long after she stopped treating me. Because of Jo's devotion to my healing and the possibil-ity of the group helping all of us to heal, she spent hours and hours on the phone, both explaining about other head injuries as well as about group process. The more we talked, the clearer my role with other head-injured people became. The more we talked, the more my role became one of compassion and understanding no matter what the injury was. I knew everyone could heal themselves just as I was doing. I had to discover how to behave with respect and love for their healing process. When Jo stopped working with me, my friend, Ruth Howe, continued to explain meanings of the group process'. (January 10 1998)

As I listened week after week to the group members, I felt a need to impose a struc-ture to the process. Members were interrupting each other and voices were being raised. I suggested that each member take turns and, with Alice's support that I be a timekeeper of sorts. I also said there could not be shouting in the group if I were to remain the leader. These expectations prompted phone calls from a few of the group members. The members explained it was because I was not head-injured that these rules were necessary. While I validated that was the way the member saw it, I also explained that the limits were necessary to my participation as facilitator. I began to see my role emerge as a boundary keeper and interpreter.

As the group continued to meet, a format emerged of introductions by storytell-ing – how the injury occurred and how I came to facilitate the group. This structure was retained although the group membership changed and a variety of activities were introduced by Alice. These activities included writing, drawing, reading poetry, discussing books read in common and singing. Alice's intelligence and creativity brought forth new activities week after week. Some weeks we only talked about members' concerns related to performance. I commented on the usefulness of the activities from the perspectives Alice raised, such as improving memory and self-expression.

After each session I listened to audiotapes of the group and looked for trends in the conversations. From this narrative analysis, themes emerged (Schwartzberg, 1994). We spent time in the group discussing the themes and my perceptions. By framing the group conversation in themes, the members felt their stories were heard, validated, and accepted. As Alice observed:

> *As they let go, with being heard, and being loved and accepted as they were, the members got their humanity back. They were empowered to begin to create a life which was different from what their lives were before.*

I was vigilant in my efforts to create a safe climate by supporting those who chose not to participate and bridging gaps in the conversation when there were distractions. I consistently expected members to take turns and attend the group, always asking about absences and lateness.

My ideas about therapy were transformed by my experience. As an occupational therapy student in the late 1960s, I was mostly educated in a medical model. By listening to members, I learned of their experience and how they were dehumanised by symptom-based thinking. This is what Alice was able to say in a poem.

Having a Head Injury Means Never Knowing What is True
It is true the experts want to help me?
It looks as if they are
looking for love
by being respected for what
they imagine they know

It looks as if they love
being respected in
their role of helping others
no matter how they do it
no matter how they harm
even themselves.

It looks as if they are
full of themselves
full of what others like them
think reality is and
believe can be done

It looks as if they are
afraid of us
who are different

Who know what is real
who know what is true
about life
about love

It looks as if
they want to know
but
are too afraid to ask
because
they have already
written in the charts
told the insurance companies
and the judges
what is wrong with us

WHAT IS TO BE EXPECTED FROM US
WE WHO ARE HEAD INJURED
WE WHO CANNOT FOCUS

LIKE THEY CAN
WE WHO CANNOT REMEMBER
QUICKLY LIKE THEY CAN

WE WHO COULD NOT KEEP
A JOB LIKE THEIRS
GOD FORBID THEY HAD AN INJURY
AND COULD NOT REMEMBER LIKE US

Alice Adelman Lowenstein

I learned to listen fully to the members and to compromise in blending their wishes with my observations and responses. This shift coincided with curriculum changes being made in my academic department and how we were teaching students. Group members came to my classes and students were free to visit or work with the peer support group. Students co-lead the group with Alice in my absence. They talked with members and wrote papers about their experience. A dialogue ensued. Students started to think person first and to really listen before making judgements. The experience of participating in this community group was dramatically different from learning in a hospital or outpatient clinic. Students and I learned to respect the politics preventing personal growth and engaged in collaborative relationships that empowered the caregivers and recipients.

Without Alice's energy, support and drive, the group would have been static. My interventions came from clinical judgement and sensitivity to my own survival needs in the group. More importantly, I had faith in the members. I grew to love them and we laughed and cried together.

DISCUSSION: FROM ALICE'S PERSPECTIVE

I needed the group because first of all, I had a dream of having other people stand up and speak with me. Secondly, I had no idea what a real injury was. Because what everybody said, first of all, was looking from the outside not from the inside. They would list the nature of what the symptoms were, but it wasn't related to what I was experiencing. So I needed the group for that. That's why people came. When I stopped needing to have the group, nobody came. Nobody called.

What I understand is this: whatever groups are formed, they will be to teach other students so that others will be treated right and with love. So, we need a leader who is a survivor. That's the vision and then we have to trust that the universe will send us the people we can handle. But look what happened, you know how many millions are out there with the need. The need is tremendous. What we've got, one after the other, people need.

DISCUSSION: FROM SHARAN'S PERSPECTIVE

It doesn't matter if you're in London, East London or Oxford. If you find the vitality of a group of people that you can connect with, that is the difference in creating a support group. The aim is to compose a group of people who can talk to each other about their head injury, the experience of head injury, and with someone who has a great need for that connection with a head injury. That's what we need. And then somebody who will be a facilitator and go on this journey like I did to discover the group. Discover the power of that small group. This is how I imagine it in my mind. It is the group who are the people who eventually become the caregivers.

CONCLUSIONS

Alice sums up the reasoning behind the support group.

Head injury experiences are different states of consciousness. If people can name it, that becomes common knowledge. Just think how this can help all these other people like those who have heart transplants. Individuals who have had journeys that don't have a head injury, but they experienced it. But, because it's not described around them, they don't know how to name it.

WHAT HAPPINESS IS OR WHAT IS FUN NOW: PART I

Eleven years after a car accident which nearly killed me, happiness and fun are very different from how they were when I was ordinary, before. I live this life, these 11 years based upon what I experienced after I lived. It's not that I don't have everything that was in my brain from the old knowing, it's just that I live with an awareness of how death makes everything I used to think was important vanish as if it never existed. Making sure that I was wearing the right clothes; I care about what I am wearing, I love clothes, but they're a costume for a task – they are not the me I am creating. I don't like being like a child dressing up as if the clothes could somehow create what I wasn't creating. The right clothes for the task, for the role, are necessary so that others believe you are who you say you are. But I don't become someone else because of what I am wearing.

I am always me. The memory of seeing how my children felt, what they thought as I would change from being real to being in my role, lingers with me. The remorse I wanted to avoid lingers behind every moment of every day. The memory of not being able to move my body lingers with me. The weeks and weeks of giving my body commands with no result linger. Years and years of not knowing where the end of my body was remain in my awareness.

The first way I am happy is when I open my eyes and see I am awake, alive in Alice's body. I am Alice's life. I am still creating Alice's life. I died and evaluated my life. I saw everything I could not change. My life was over. I argued with the beings. God, the-all-knowing-all-loving-power-of-creation, had forgiven me, loved me even though I was imperfect, even though in the life before, I was unaware I was on a journey of the spirit. Jeffrey's mother's body, Michael's mother's body, Jonathan's mother's body, a woman's body, a mother's body, an athlete's body, a body which has served me well is to feel where my body ends. I feel air on my skin. My awareness has the form of my body after so many years without. I am thankful my soul has become reconnected with my body. Any movement, any small movement like moving back in a chair or turning my head makes me aware what a blessing it is to have a body which functions. What my body could not do lingers in my awareness. The years of losing it when I coughed or laughed or farted, the inability to control what was, shamed me. Years of not knowing what my body was saying.

WHAT HAPPINESS IS OR WHAT IS FUN NOW: PART II

Walking is happiness
    one foot after the other
        in balance without falling
        without tripping
        walking safely
        not being in danger of falling over

That's what happiness is

Happiness is knowing I can wait to go to the bathroom
    Knowing I can depend upon my body
        to wait
        not to shame me
    every time I laugh
        every time I cough
            every time I sneeze

Happiness is knowing
    I am Alive
        in Alice's body

which had Alice's children
   Alice's friends

Happiness is wanting to move
   and my body doing it

Each day I am reminded
   how happy I am with my body

Happiness is the pleasure of mastery
   the pleasure of walking
      forwards
      backwards

Picking up my feet so I don't trip
   sideways
   around in circles
however I want to move

Happiness is breaking into a run

Happiness is sitting in a chair
   without pain or muscle spasms

Happiness is swimming

Happiness is moving my arms
   in all the ways arms move
      or at least most of the ways

Happiness is moving my body
   in the memory of old movements
      skillfully with mastery
      as an athlete
      as a dancer

Happiness is walking down stairs
   one leg and then the other
      on alternate steps

without having to hold on
   with two hands
      going backwards
      like a child
      keeping herself safe

Happiness is hearing what people are saying
  even though there is background noise

Happiness is being able to concentrate
  despite background noise

Happiness is knowing
  my clothes fit

Knowing I can put them on
  myself
  without help

Happiness is knowing
  I can pay my bills
when I need to

Knowing I can add and subtract
  consciously

Happiness is knowing
  my brain adds and subtracts
and tells me what I can and can't buy

Happiness is knowing
  I am on a spiritual journey
  I seem to be different from most people
  They love being distracted
from what I am conscious of
  They love going into other worlds
in movies, in books, in songs
  anything to take them
out of their worlds

Alice Lowenstein
June 22 1997
Brookline, Massachusetts, USA

Further thoughts

1 Reviewing Alice's poetry, how does it help your understanding of Alice and what are the implications for you as a professional?
2 The group, not the therapist, identifies a range of activities. Why is this important?

3 Focusing on the participant role of Sharan and her students, discuss how this role differs from a 'therapy' role.
4 What are the different learning methods which could facilitate understanding of illness and recovery?

REFERENCES

Schwartzberg, S. L. (1994) Helping factors in a peer developed support group for persons with head injury. Part 1: A participant observer view. *American Journal of Occupational Therapy*, 48(4), 297–304.

SECTION THREE _____

INTERACTIONAL AND EDUCATIONAL APPLICATIONS

8 INTERACTING AND COLLABORATING IN PRACTICE

Mary Jenkins

KEY POINTS
- Rehabilitation – cerebrovascular accident
- Context
- Democratic practice – a contract of equals
- Interactional analysis

The focus of this chapter examines the systematic analysis of practitioner and client interactions. The author posits that occupational therapy practice has always had at its core the 'client', arguing that, as a result, practice has become a democratic learning experience for both the client and the therapist. She describes the negotiation of practice which takes place between the two so that the client's unique perspective and way of being is central. The conclusion suggests that the duality in this negotiated practice differs from that of Schon's (1987) notion of 'expert knowledge'. Working in this way she believes occupational therapists can assume a pioneering role in health and social care.

OCCUPATIONAL THERAPY AND CONTEXT

It is my personal view that context is especially important in the field of occupational therapy. I suggest that the contextualist world view offered by Jaeger and Rosnow (1988), which states that 'the world is events', is worthy of comment here. In their opinion an event is an individual action of everyday life that is set in time and consists of a combination of factors, relations and activities in a state of perpetual motion. Essentially, what they are saying is that events are experiences; they cannot happen in a vacuum but only in a context. Thus, the interrelationship between an event and its context is fundamental and is the avenue by which meaning is conferred. Bhaskar's remark 'To think of contexts as existing in addition to or apart from practices is like imagining smiles alongside or beside faces' (1983, p. 87) makes the argument explicitly – without context there is no meaning. This is the centrepoint of occupational therapy.

Occupational therapy stresses the integralness of the person in the world as an active participant member. My own work (1994) confirms the profession as a personalised service contiguous with clients' lifeworld contexts, wherein that practice is concerned with situational problems and with the need for interactants, both clients and practitioners, to generate personally relevant theory to understand these. It is, in fact, a vital and rich learning ground for both interactants and it has a humanist approach. The practitioner enters the client's domain and attempts to view the illness through his/her eyes. It is notably client centred, unlike the traditional medical approach in which practitioners try to bring the client's illness into their world and to interpret the illness in terms of biomedicine, this focus being described by McWhinney (1985) as practitioner centred.

The contextualist view offers an alternative vision, a practice world which respects both client and practitioner input and impact. Balint (1961) and Engel (1977) were among the first physicians to realise and publicly expose the inadequacies of the traditional medical model in reaching any deep understanding of the person's illness. The dilemma was acknowledged by Cassell (1985) who writes:

The story of an illness – the patient's history – has two protagonists, the body and the person. By careful questioning it is possible to separate out the facts that speak of disturbed bodily functions, the pathophysiology that gives you the diagnosis. To do this, the facts about the body's dysfunction must be separated from the meaning that the patient has attached to them. Skilled physicians have been doing this for ages. All too often, however, the personal meanings are then discarded. With them go the doctor's opportunity to know who the patient is. (p. 108)

A HUMANIST APPROACH

The process of occupational therapy demands a different approach. From the outset the discipline awarded pride of place to the client. It grew out of the philanthropic ideals of middle Americans at the start of the 20th century and it filled a gap in medical treatment initially mooted by Meyer (1922), i.e. the conception of health problems as problems of living and not simply as medical conditions. Mock, as early as 1919, noted: 'Occupational therapists are interested in answers to questions about how people learn. They are concerned with human motivation . . .' (p. 13). The potency of such beliefs is described by a client:

You're coming to talk to the soul of the person, whereas others have dealt with the leg or whatever you know you are getting to the inner person. (Jenkins, 1994, p. 240).

This form of relationship is in stark contrast to the emotional neutrality of Parsons (1951) and claimed by him for the medical profession and subsequently all allied professions. The notion of affect in the client/practitioner encounter has been discouraged but at a cost. Zimmerman suggests it has led to a 'dehumanising effect upon students and health practitioners' (1974, p. 467).

In occupational therapy, in contrast to other professions, a model of mutual participation has always existed, though this may have been somewhat diluted when the discipline was caught up in the drive for scientification. Yerxa (1980), co-founder of the occupational science movement, saw the situation as a move from humanism to scientism to a society dominated by technique.

A LEARNING GROUND

It is proposed in this chapter that the concept of professional knowledge is not assumed as a result of formal training *per se*, but rather is determined through practice. This practice, in my view, has four components: access, language, community and context (Jenkins and Brotherton, 1995). Context as discussed earlier is the enveloping dimension. Access and language are the primary ingredients and community allows the learning to take place. The result is a practice experience which presents opportunities for learning for all interactants. Its richness is infinite and the process mutually respectful and collaborative. Knowledge derived in this manner is a shared experience with and for the client and cannot become a tool to be used unthinkingly. When this practice experience happens, encounters have been shown to be more successful (Kleinman *et al.*, 1978; Morgan and Engel, 1969; Quill, 1983, Stewart, 1974).

It is my contention that client orientation in occupational therapy is not only the basis of the profession but is the catalyst. This enables practitioners to interact wholly with clients, increasing involvement density and priming and the transaction for reciprocity. I use these terms 'involvement density', 'priming' and 'the transaction for reciprocity' because they say exactly what is happening; the significance of affect for engagement has long been established.

At the macro level this situatedness is aptly described:

> *Occupational therapy has been superb in clients with functional disabilities after a stroke. No other group can overcome the patient with haemianopia, with neglect, with dysfunction of the upper limb. Perfect input. That to me is a classic example where they (occupational therapists) have done the assessment, picked up the problem, identified and worked out a management structure. At each stage outcome is reassessed and presented to other allied professionals, then translated into functional improvements in dressing, in kitchen work, etc. Finally, follow-up in the community, what aids and adaptations need provided and subsequently follow-up on an outpatient basis. That has absolutely no medical input, very little physiotherapy input, a clear example of occupational therapy doing good. (Jenkins, 1994, p. 249)*

This work insists that occupational therapy goes beyond this lived-out reality, offering a truly democratic experience that affords client equality.

This is demonstrated at the micro level in the encounter between occupational therapist and client. In exposing the client and practitioner interaction to analysis, it is possible to assess the nature of the occupational therapy encounter and to access the interdynamics and interdependencies of the practice situation in context. The example presented is from my own doctoral work (Jenkins, 1994).

INTERACTION ANALYSIS

Systematic analysis of practitioner–client interaction is relatively new. Most studies have been based on the doctor–patient encounter. For my study, the chief concern was to find an interactional analysis system which provided a way of describing the therapeutic process at a relatively whole level as opposed to a constituent level and one that was capable of measuring the interactional relationship from both interactants' perspectives. The only interactional analysis system affording this was Roter *et al.*'s framework (1988). It consists of six communication categories for practitioners and five categories for patients which are listed below.

Six practitioner categories		Five patient categories
1. Information giving	(IG)	Information giving
2. Information seeking	(IS)	Information seeking
3. Social conversation	(SC)	Social conversation
4. Positive talk	(PT)	Positive talk
5. Negative talk	(NT)	Negative talk
6. Partnership building	(PB)	

In applying the framework to the occupational therapy encounter, two amendments were made:

1 that described as social conversation was revised to refer to courtesy talk only;
2 a sixth variable, partnership building, was added to include those client behaviours demonstrating partnership and sharing.

Figure 8.1 is an extract from the recorded interaction and shows a sample of discourse coding. In analysis each verbal unit is numbered and categorised. When using passages from the encounter this information will be included. (A transcript of the whole event is obtainable from the author.)

THE ENCOUNTER

The practitioner is aged 33. She obtained a Diploma in Occupational Therapy and more recently a BSc in Professional Development. She worked in a general physical hospital before moving into the community as a senior therapist. She is presently a practitioner and manager of elderly services. The client, A, is aged 66 years. He is a retired heating engineer and lives with his wife in a single-storey dwelling. He had a right CVA in January 1992 and as a result has left-sided weakness. In February 1993 he incurred a fracture of the right neck of femur. This was treated by insertion of a dynamic hip screw; he had five treatment sessions in occupational therapy from 2nd to 9th March 1993. The recorded treatment session presented here is number 5.

At the beginning of the session the practitioner immediately situates action and establishes the client's lifeworld.

Verbal Unit			Discourse Coding
85	C	*Now what do you want me to do?*	IS
116	P	*I want to see how you can manage to get that cup onto the table.*	IG
117	P	*If it's difficult, A, there's a wee trolley just behind we can try you with.*	IG
86	C	*Aye.*	PT
118	P	*But we'll just try this way first and see how it goes.*	IG
87			
119	P	*What way do you do it with L?*	IS
88	C	*I don't think I did take it onto the table.*	IG
120	P	*She did it for you?*	IS
89	C	*I don't think . . .*	IG
121	P	*Just try and don't worry if it's going to spill, we'll get it sorted for you.*	PT
90	C	*My hands are shaking, you see, it still shakes from the stroke you know.*	IG
122	P	*Uhuh, I know that.*	PB
91	C	*Both the hands shake.*	IG
123	P	*If you think it is going to spill, A, don't risk it, I'll give you a trolley.*	IG
92	C	*Aye, OK, give me the trolley.*	IG
124	P	*Will we try that?*	IS

P = Practitioner, C = Client

Figure 8.1

A sample of discourse coding.

1	P	*You know you did it last week.*
1	C	*Yes.*
2	P	*More practice moving around the kitchen and also things like bending down to the fridge and getting the milk.*
2	C	*I was.*
11	P	*How does this compare with your kitchen at home?*
6	C	*Ahh, hhm! It's about the same size.*
12	P	*Right, we'll have a look at maybe today how you manage to get the cup from the worktop over to the table or if you need to use one of the wee trolleys.*
7	C	*Yes, ahh, no, I didn't need to use a trolley, I used to carry [pause] I only had a stick, you see the last time. I used to carry.*
13	P	*Uhuh, given you have this walking frame at the minute.*
8	C	*I don't know how I'll get on with that.*
14	P	*Sure now, we'll give it a go anyway and see how you get on.*
9	C	*OK.*

Here context is primary but also note the accessibility of the therapist to the client's perspective. There is an open-endedness to the repartee without the practitioner taking a dogmatic approach, The client has his say and his concern is duly regarded. As the session goes on he is allowed to exercise control.

19	P	*You can either do it through the lid or take the lid off.*
14	C	*Off.*
20	P	*You're making it more difficult for yourself.*
15	C	*I know, well, that's the way I do it at home so.*
21	P	*Right, OK that's it.*

This extract demonstrates full client participation. The interchange between interactants is respectful and the practitioner accepts the client's way of doing things. She does not exert an 'I know better' authority and continues to invite him to take ownership of the event in her use of language.

29	P	*Now, you either sit or stand while that's to boil or do you want to go and sit down?*
22	C	*I'll stand just till it boils, I'll get this here ready.*
30	P	*Do you want to get your cup and things all out there?*
23	C	*I'll get this here ready, the cooker.*
31	P	*Right. [pause]*
32	P	*Right you are.*
33	P	*Do you want it that high?*
24	C	*No, I want it low.*

And later:

57	C	*Right, aye, wait till we see where we are now.*
58	C	*Will I do it exactly the same as I'd do it at home?*
86	P	*Yip.*
87	P	*So, if you put it on to boil for a long time at home, do exactly that.*
59	C	*I have to do something else first.*
88	P	*What?*
60	C	*Warm the pot.*
89	P	*Now, do you usually do this at home with the flex in, A?*
61	C	*Uhuh!*
90	P	*Right, OK just thought maybe – it's easier with it out but it's up to you.*

Here there is a sense of a community of practice wherein the client is encouraged to take responsibility and practice is markedly two-way. In this instance the practitioner permits the client to make decisions about the appropriateness of his actions. This approach pays dividends in that he does acknowledge as treatment progresses when he needs to change his behaviour in the circumstances for safety and convenience. The example presented in Figure 8.1 is used again here to illustrate the genuine democratic process in which neither party forces their opinion or insists on an acceptance of their viewpoint.

85	C	*Now what do you want me to do?*
116	P	*I want to see how you can manage to get that cup onto the table. [pause]*
117	P	*If it's difficult, A, there's a wee trolley just behind we can try you with.*
86	C	*Aye.*
118	P	*But we'll just try this way first and see how it goes.*
87	C	*Now to see.*
119	P	*What way did you do it with L?*
88	C	*I don't think I did take it onto the table.*
120	P	*She did it for you.*
89	C	*I don't think . . .*
121	P	*Just try and don't worry if it's going to spill, we'll get it sorted for you.*
90	C	*My hands are shaking, you see, it still shakes from the stroke, you know.*
122	P	*Uhuh, I know that.*
91	C	*Both the hands shake.*
123	P	*If you think it is going to spill, A, don't risk it, I'll give you a trolley.*
92	C	*Aye, OK, give me the trolley.*
124	P	*Will we try that?*

The practitioner invites the client to do things his way. She does not presume superior knowledge of his ability or dictate the steps of action. She works with the client as he makes his own discoveries. Not only is the therapist in the transaction developing views of the client and her treatment, the client is developing an appreciation of his own abilities and limitations. The practitioner is quick to build on the positive choices, as is indicated here.

129	P	*If you had to have one of these at home, what we could do is not use the zimmer too much in the kitchen and use this because it's the same thing – you can put two hands on it and move around . . .*

There is a sense of camaraderie, in which both players are targeting the same goal. The interplay demonstrates the evolutionary nature of knowledge growth and understanding amongst interactants. It does more, it shows a degree of reciprocity and intercourse which only exists when players attend to each other, when communication is, in fact, affective and effective and when their learning has been done in the context of practice – a context which is not divorced from the client's lifeworld. At that moment in time it is the client's lifeworld context, as dynamic as any event, evolving and changing as the process of occupational therapy itself, as described by Jenkins and Brotherton (1995) who state that:

> *Occupational therapists do not simply look at the stroke patient, the actual presenting symptoms, they actually look at the patient, where they're coming from and where they're going to. (p. 332)*

This factor was one of the reasons for changing the variable social conversation to courtesy talk. The siting of home and family circumstances adds 'a real, as it is' dimension to the client and impacts on treatment as shown in this excerpt.

165	P	*Do you normally do the washing up at home or do you leave it?*
118	C	*No, I leave them.*
166	P	*Aye, why did I think that? [laughing]*
167	C	*Sometimes I would do them if I had time; like you know; it takes me two hours to make my breakfast. When I waken I have orange juice first.*
167	P	*Hm!*
120	C	*Then I have All-Bran.*
168	P	*Right.*
121	C	*Then I have two rounds of toast.*
168	P	*Uhuh.*
122	C	*And.*
170	P	*Well, L did the toast with you the last day and there was no problem because it was all high up.*
123	C	*That's right.*
171	P	*The main thing is how to reach down to the fridge. That's why I want to make a cup of tea today.*

The practitioner clearly states her reasoning for the activity, ensuring the client's involvement in the procedure. Towards the end of treatment time, the practitioner wished to allow some more practice in dressing, particularly the lower half of his body, given concerns about damaging the new hip joint.

262	P	*Right, just like you did with that lace, you did it very well so what I thought we'd put that shoe on to give you a chance to see if you can tie it yourself without putting the elastic lace in and if not, we'll try the elastic one.*
190	C	*OK. Right.*
263	P	*There's a shoe horn there if you want it. [pause]*
264	P	*Just take your time, don't worry if it doesn't . . . I think it's going to. [pause]*
265	P	*Well done! You did it.*
191	C	*Mm. Mm.*
266	P	*Isn't that the first time you did that since your fall, isn't it?*
192	C	*Yeah! I think it is.*
267	P	*So the main thing, still don't cross your legs over or do anything . . .*
193	C	*No, I don't.*
268	P	*That's still in the limits of safety and does mean you're able to do it yourself.*
194	C	*Hm, yes.*
269	P	*That's great.*

270 P *In fact, if you can do it yourself it's better than elastic laces because some of the problems, A, is the tongue of your shoe sometimes catches.*

197 C *Yes, yes.*

Here the practitioner enters the life of the client, eliciting and giving information about the disablement within the context of that person; a situation which, according to Mishler (1984), is foreign to medical interviews. He argues that typical interactions between doctors and patients are doctor-centred, dominated as he says by a technocratic perspective and not the humanistic perspective which has punctuated this interaction. By way of emphasising this, it is pertinent to note the way the practitioner advised the client.

46 P *Now of the things you're doing not really safe is standing there and leaning over the zimmer.*

54 P *If you like you can turn this around, you can use both hands then.*

63 P *I just want to show you, just step over here a wee bit, just leave the zimmer like that.*

   C *Uhuh!*

64 P *And you can actually put one hand on the worktop if you want to stabilise yourself a bit more and then reach down.*

207 P *Just, A, when you're throwing it down make it easier for yourself, you see there.*

219 P *That should be OK, just give it a good hard pull, A, and that will take it out over your heel.*

247 P *You know the way I showed you – throw it down, A.*

   C *Uhuh.*

248 P *That's it!*

249 P *See, can you do it without me holding it this time?*

The reciprocity evidenced in these exchanges pinpoints the elements of access and language which, as has already been stated, are central to the democratic practice being advocated. Another characteristic of the encounter is how the practitioner has been careful to ensure that throughout the transaction the client is fully aware of what's happening.

177 P *Just before you go, what we are going to do now, A, is just to go back in there and sit on the bench to have another run through your socks because that was a wee bit difficult this morning.*

274 P *Right, what we're going to do tomorrow morning, A, is put you on again for dressing practice.*

280 P *And whenever you're ready to go home or when any discharge date is set, we'll do a visit, probably just the day you go home.*

A POWER SHIFT

The model of professional practice emerging from this sample encounter marks a shift in the balance and sharing of power between the professional and the client. The shift is notable in both verbal and non-verbal behaviour. From field notes, observer A remarks:

> *Throughout the whole session the practitioner was in close proximity behind the patient moving with him and at the same time allowing him space to go in any direction. She used a lot of eye contact with the patient and always bent down to face the patient when giving instructions, directions or forms of encouragement as 'that's right', 'good', 'that's it'. Positive words such as these were frequently used in conjunction with nodding and smiling. Touch was used when the therapist was helping to stabilise objects, e.g. the kettle or the sock, or helping the patient to move if sitting down or demonstrating the zimmer (walking frame).*

Observer Z's report notes:

> *The occupational therapist gave encouragement and praise to the patient when appropriate but placed him under no pressure or obligation to do things he did not want to do . . . The flow of conversation was constant throughout the inter-action, there were no uneasy pauses. Although the practitioner's speech was very fast, the patient was able to comprehend and if he was unsure, he was not afraid to ask.*

This democratic community of practice has the following features. Partnership and negotiation between professional and client have been seen to occur here in practice, through events in which practitioner and client learned together of the possibilities and limitations of interventions. It would seem that power, a characteristic of traditional professionalism, is replaced with caring – a caring which urges the professional to recognise, to make central in theory and practice the individuality of the person receiving the service. The byproduct is the creation of a learning environment that is complementary in nature, where there is circulation of knowledge and information among interactants, a sharing of understandings and opportunities for participation at all levels. The result is a community of practice similar to Lave and Wenger's concept of 'a set of relations among persons, activity, and world, over time and in relation with other, tangential and overlapping communities-of-practice' (1989, p. 24). This differs from Schon's notion of a community of practitioners: 'Through countless acts of attention and inattention, naming, sense making, boundary setting and control, they make and maintain the worlds matched to their professional knowledge and know-how' (1987, p. 36), wherein the emphasis is their expert knowledge. Here the emphasis is the evolutionary nature and mutuality of knowledge and understanding.

There is a democracy about this professionalism which features collaboration with clients, significant others and carers in treatment and an appreciation of client situations and viewpoints as a knowledge base for practice, rather than viewing them incidentally and indifferently. The importance of an affective bond between practitioner and client is obvious.

Many argue that professionals, for their survival, must work with their clientele utilising the knowledge of both the practitioner and the client in the encounter. Jenkins (1998) cites 'the self' as the critical factor. When the self is blinded by either professional elitism or personal disengagement, the encounter is not effective. The findings of my study support Haug's (1977) contention that expert knowledge is not enough and its demise is at hand. Ideally, the transaction should be a contract of equals – a bargaining mechanism which results in negotiated approaches to care. The evidence presented does suggest that occupational therapy is now mature as a profession alongside medicine but also offers a pioneer democratic professionalism. What the future holds for us is what we hold for the future. The invitation to us is to do or die.

Further thoughts

1 Focusing on your practice context, consider the interactions which you have with a particular client. Identify ways in which your treatment acknowledges their unique perspective.
2 Using the adapted framework (Roter) outlined in the chapter, record either a treatment or supervision session. Select a 10-minute section and analyse the verbal units to identify if any democratic interactions are occurring. If not, identify how these could be created in future sessions.
3 How does this systematic analysis of interaction relate to or add to interactional reasoning?

REFERENCES

Balint, M. (1961) The other part of medicine. *Lancet*, 1, 40–42.
Bhaskar, R. (1983) Beef, structure and place: notes from a critical naturalist perspective. *Journal for the Theory of Social Behaviour*, 11, 81–97.
Cassell, E. J. (1985) *Talking with Patients. Vol. 2: Clinical Technique*. MIT Press, Cambridge, MA.
Engel, G. L. (1977) The need for a new medical model: a challenge for biomedicine, *Science*, 196, 129–136.
Haug, M. (1977) Computer technology and the obsolescence of the concept of profession. In M. R. Haug and Dofny (eds) *Work and Technology*. Sage, Beverly Hills, CA.
Jaeger, M. E., Rosnow, R. L. (1988) Contextualism and its implications for psychological inquiry. *British Journal of Psychology*, 79, 63–75.
Jenkins, M. M. (1994) Occupational therapy – perspectives on the effectiveness of practice. PhD Thesis, University of Ulster, Magee.
Jenkins, M. M. (1998) Shifting ground or sifting sand? Occupational therapy – a

democratic profession. In J. Creek (ed.) *Critical Essays on Aspects of Occupational Therapy and Philosophy*. Whurr Publications, London.

Jenkins, M. M., Brotherton, C. (1995) In search of a theoretical framework for practice, part 2. *British Journal of Occupational Therapy*, 58, 332–336.

Kleinman, A., Eisenberg, L., Good, B. (1978) Culture, illness and care: clinical lessons from anthropologic and cross-cultural research. *Annals of Internal Medicine*, 88, 251–258.

Lave, J., Wenger, E. (1989) Situated Learning; Legitimate Peripheral Participation. Report No. IRL 89-0013. Institute for Research on Learning, Palo Alto, CA, pp. 1–41.

McWhinney, I. R. (1985) Patient-centred and doctor-centred models of clinical decision making. In M. Sheldon, J. Brooke and A. Rector (eds) *Decision Making in General Practice*. Stockton Press, New York, pp. 31–46.

Meyer, A. (1922) The philosophy of occupational therapy. *Archives of Occupational Therapy*, 1, 1–10.

Mishler, E. G. (1984) *The Discourse of Medicine: Dialectics of Medical Interviews*. Ablex, Norwood, NJ.

Mock, H. E. (1919) Curative work. *Carry On*, 1, 12–17.

Morgan, W. L., Engel, G. L. (1969) *The Clinical Approach to the Patient*, W. B. Saunders, Philadelphia.

Parsons, T. (1951) Social structure and dynamic process: the case of modern medical practice. In *The Social System*. The Free Press, New York, pp. 428–279.

Quill, T. E. (1983) Partnerships in patient care: a contractual approach. *Annals of Internal Medicine*, 98, 228–234.

Roter, D. L., Hall, J. A., Katz, N. R. (1988) Patient–physician communication: a descriptive summary of the literature. *Patient Education and Counselling*, 99–119.

Schon, D. A. (1987) *Educating the Reflective Practitioner*. Jossey-Bass, San Francisco.

Stewart, M. (1974) Comments on Ebel's paper. The logic of the aptitude achievement distinction. In D. R. Green (ed.) *The Aptitude Achievement Distinction*. CTB/McGraw-Hill, Monterey, California.

Yerxa, E. J. (1980) Occupational therapy's role in creating a future climate of caring. *American Journal of Occupational Therapy*, 34, 529–534.

Zimmerman, T. (1974) Is professionalisation the answer to improving health care? *American Journal of Occupational Therapy*, 28, 465–468.

9 MAKING CHANGES: A CLINICAL REASONING JOURNEY

Matthew Molineux

KEY POINTS
- Personal meaning
- Understanding clients' stories
- Fieldwork education
- Adult learning theories
- Transforming practice

The personal story told here forms a journey of discovery for Matthew as his under-standing and the significance of clinical reasoning knowledge develop. He highlights how he changed his own way of working in his service. This experience was used in conjunction with other educators to develop a different fieldwork experience for a group of first-year students. Strategies implemented with these students are described and their effect on the students' learning experience discussed. He relates how narrative has become a central tool in his work.

INTRODUCTION

In the last few years clinical reasoning has played a significant part in my profes-sional life as an occupational therapy clinician, manager and educator. It has informed and enriched my practice in many ways and some of this I hope to share in this chapter. In retrospect, one of the key concepts which I have taken from clinical reasoning is that of narrative, the idea that human beings use stories to make sense of the world and their experiences in that world. This chapter will tell the story of my experiences of clinical reasoning.

First, as you can already see, this chapter is written in the first person. It is true that writing from this perspective is slowly becoming more widely accepted, although there are some who continue to argue vehemently against this style. While I agree that there are some contexts in which this writing style would be inappropri-ate, this chapter is certainly not one of those. As I have already stated, it is my hope to share my experiences of clinical reasoning. Given that I have used stories or nar-ratives to make sense of these experiences for myself, it seems appropriate that I share my stories with you. The second characteristic of this chapter, which will be difficult for some academics to accept, is that the stories which make up this chapter will be just that and as such are not replete with references to learned papers and writers. Key works will, however, be cited.

There are three sections to the following chapter which are smaller episodes within my overall story of clinical reasoning, the end of which is not yet written. The first section will describe how I first became aware of, struggled with and later used clinical reasoning principles. This section will describe the postgraduate MSc programme I was undertaking when I first studied clinical reasoning and my first attempts at using this new knowledge. The second section is the focus of this chapter. It will describe the pilot research study I was involved in which used principles of clinical reasoning to structure a fieldwork education placement for four students. This section will include details of how the project began, the structure of the placement and the results of the evaluation. The final section will briefly outline how I have used my knowledge of clinical reasoning since this project and, indeed, how I continue to use it. While the focus of this chapter is the fieldwork education programme, I believe it is important for you to have some appreciation of how it came to be and what has happened since – how it fits within my overall story. Let us begin.

CLINICAL REASONING . . . NOW I GET IT!

Getting there

I arrived in the United Kingdom in April 1993, having planned, with a group of friends from university, to work and travel for about one year, something many Australian occupational therapists seem to do. I began work as a locum in London and had several jobs interspersed with two bouts of travelling. Towards the end of 1993 I began as a locum in acute orthopaedics in Newham, the most easterly borough of London. This post proved more challenging than I had anticipated. Orthopaedics was not new to me as my first job after graduating was a six-month post on an acute ward in a teaching hospital. However, here I noticed a sharp contrast. In this position, it seemed that all I was valued for was the equipment I could provide so that people could be discharged home, in order for beds to be cleared. My preregistration education had instilled in me the value and the power of occupation and so I became increasingly frustrated by the situation in which I found myself. The post of head occupational therapist for the team I was working in was vacant. I received tremendous support from another head occupational therapist and the occupational therapy service manager and the three of us tried to make changes whenever and wherever we could. Unfortunately there was little change and I was becoming more and more frustrated and professionally demoralised.

The desire to change the situation drove me to apply for the vacant position and so I became the head occupational therapist for that team. During my time in that position the health service underwent many changes and as a result so did the trust I was working in and the team I was managing. Through these changes it became a community and mental health services trust and included all mental health services, therapy services, district nursing and most services for children in the borough.

Contracts and service level agreements formed the basis of working between our trust and the local acute services trust. The team I managed became known as the occupational therapy service for adults, a service for people aged 16–65 years whose difficulties in occupational performance were due primarily to a physical condition. Our service worked with inpatients, outpatients and people living in the community, which meant that we were able to provide an integrated service, i.e. one in which source of referral or location of the client did not dictate service provision. Our team of occupational therapists, assistants and technicians saw people with a variety of conditions including, stroke, cancer, HIV/AIDS, spinal injuries, multiple sclerosis, fractures, back injuries, amputations and chronic obstructive airways disease.

While I was enjoying my new role and all the challenges it included, I wanted more intellectual stimulation. I was also beginning to consider my longer term career plans and this had always included becoming an occupational therapy educator. Postgraduate study seemed one option open to me and around this time I became aware of the fairly new course at the University of East London led by Susan Ryan. After speaking to a current student and meeting with Susan, I decided to apply to the course and I was accepted. One of the deciding factors in choosing this course was that it led to a MSc in Occupational Therapy which matched my desire to pursue further study focused on occupational therapy. I also had the impression from talking to others about the course that I would be encouraged to think differently about my profession and my place within it. It is worth saying that the philosophy of the entire programme was very much based on principles of adult learning and reflection, but also that one of the expected outcomes of the programme was that participants would act as agents of professional change. This was particularly appealing to me given my thoughts about current practice. I began the course in September 1994.

The course was modular and apart from two compulsory subjects and the research dissertation, there was some freedom to choose modules of particular interest and relevance. I spent the first term studying the two compulsory modules, occupational therapy and research methods. I then chose modules in counselling and communicating, fieldwork education, an independent module on occupational science which I designed myself, and the module on clinical reasoning.

The clinical reasoning module

I undertook the clinical reasoning module in my second term, February to June 1995. The 15-week module had two distinct components, one tutor facilitated and the other student facilitated. The tutor-led sessions introduced us to the history of clinical reasoning in health professions, clinical reasoning research in occupational therapy, narrative and reflection. Four weeks at the end of the module were taken up with each participant presenting the results of their investigation into some aspect of reasoning in their own practice. A key aspect of the module involved keeping a reflective journal and recording our thoughts and feelings in this journal after each session. Admittedly, my journal was not as thoughtful and reflective as it could have been and my skills in this area have developed since then, but it was nonetheless a highly useful learning experience.

One of the themes which runs throughout my journal is, not surprisingly, that my knowledge and understanding of clinical reasoning increased during the module. However, while this is what one would expect for a postgraduate module, what is interesting is the way in which my greater appreciation came about. It was certainly not an easy process, as my journal entry of week 4 attests:

> *I had great difficulty understanding three-track reasoning, which disappointed me quite a bit as that is what occupational therapists are supposed to do – so it is very relevant to me.*

Indeed, it was not until week 11 that '. . . *finally the three-track mind and narrative make sense'*.

For me, then, understanding clinical reasoning was a task in itself and I can very clearly remember when, after reading the papers in the special edition on clinical reasoning in the *American Journal of Occupational Therapy* (November, 1991), the penny finally dropped and everything started to make sense. Narrative in particular seemed to have a real impact on me at the time and my journal has many references to this:

> *'I really like the narrative framing approach. The idea of stories makes a lot of sense, especially story making.' (Week 4)*
> *'I like very much the idea of thinking narratively . . .' (Week 7)*

My experience of coming to terms with clinical reasoning is something which has stuck in my mind and continues to affect the way I expose others to the same subject.

Another way in which I have been affected by the module, which is also clear from reading my journal, is the need to consider alternative perspectives in order to truly understand a client or a situation. For me, this was highlighted in an activity we completed in week 1 of the module which required us to watch a video of a man and to consider what it might be like to work with him. There was no sound to the video and we were given no other information. After watching the video and making some notes, we then discussed our thoughts with one other person. My journal entry captures the essence of my experience that day.

> *The discussion with [other participant] about the video of the elderly man was interesting. I focused completely on the man and observed everything I could, trying to make a diagnosis. I came up with CVA. [Other participant], on the other hand, just looked at it as a man going fishing with his friends. She made up a story about them going in the boat to an island to have a picnic. She said she could even hear the wind, smell the grass, etc. I think we were on either ends of the spectrum . . . The group discussion which followed made me realise that I am perhaps too narrow in my appreciation of a situation.*

I can still vividly recall that discussion and my amazement at the huge differences between my thoughts on the 'man in the boat' and the very elaborate and rich story told by my fellow student. Again, this idea of a narrow view of practice has had a lasting impact on me and has been something I have given great thought to since the module. I have become particularly interested in the way external factors, such as service philosophies, politics and professional domains of concern, impact on the practice of occupational therapy. What also continues to intrigue and frustrate me is the extent to which occupational therapists allow this to occur.

While the module stimulated a great deal of thinking about other issues, such as the relationship between the expert clinician and the expert at clinical reasoning, it is probably those discussed earlier which have had the most significant and lasting impact on me as an occupational therapist.

Taking it into the field

It was during the following term, while I was completing a module on fieldwork education, that Susan Ryan approached me and asked if I would be interested in participating in a pilot study to look at an approach to fieldwork education of preregistration students founded on clinical reasoning. At the time I was, as outlined earlier, a team leader with a clinical caseload and so I continued to take students on placement. I was also a clinical lecturer with the local school of occupational therapy. Susan approached Gwilym Roberts who was at the time director of fieldwork education to ask if he, and the school, would be interested in participating in the pilot. After some discussions, we all agreed and began planning a group approach to fieldwork education which was underpinned by the principles of clinical reasoning, reflection and adult learning. The planning took the form of the three of us meeting a few times to discuss the logistics of the study and some ideas for how the five-week placement would be structured. After this, I planned the five-week placement in more detail in consultation with my team members, as well as with Susan and Gwilym.

The school and the placement

The school of occupational therapy was located within what was then the London Hospital Medical College at Whitechapel in East London. It was established in 1989 and offered a two-year accelerated course to graduates which led to registration as an occupational therapist. The educational philosophy of the course emphasises adult learning and problem-based learning. During their two years, students undertake five full-time fieldwork education placements with the first one quite early in the course, only 11 weeks after starting, and it was this first placement which was chosen. The aims of this particular placement included developing:

- an understanding of the key concepts and theories underlying the provision of health and social care;
- an understanding of the assessment element of this process;
- interpersonal and professional interaction with clients, carers and colleagues (School of Occupational Therapy, 1995).

The placement programme

The programme aimed to develop students' skills and knowledge in two main areas. First, given the aims of this particular placement, was the assessment phase of the occupational therapy process, in particular initial interviews. Second was the human aspect of practice, which included the interactional skills used in working with clients, self-awareness and an appreciation of the illness experience. To this end, the design process was informed by knowledge of adult learning approaches to education and clinical reasoning. The central themes of adult learning which were particularly relevant included the use of learning contracts, adequate preparation of students, peer learning groups, emphasis on the *process* of learning, control of learning progressively turned over to students and a focus on the exploration of important concepts rather than specific knowledge (Brookfield, 1986; Ryan, 1993).

From a clinical reasoning perspective, the importance of the relationship between client and therapist and the therapist's ability to understand the client from a phenomenological perspective were seen as integral to this placement experience (Mattingly and Fleming, 1994). In addition, research into the development of reasoning skills provided much data which informed placement design.

- It has been found that student occupational therapists are better able to identify client problems after meeting the individual rather than when relying purely on referral information (Neistadt, 1987).
- Novice therapists treat clients according to general categories, follow general rules and rely on these to make decisions, are very concrete and focus on objective data, are less able to form a narrative image of the person and do not appear to integrate information from the interactional aspect of reasoning (Mattingly, 1989).
- Novice therapists have less confidence about reasoning interactively and so concentrate on the procedural aspects of reasoning (Fleming, 1991).
- Less experienced therapists have been found to be less thorough in data collection, less aware of discrepancies in information and less autonomous (Ryan, 1990).

In the interests of clarity, what follows is a week-by-week outline of the programme which highlights the main components of the placement. It should be noted that, in the light of the information provided above and in relation to the aims of the placement within the entire course, two strands ran through the placement – client contact and assessment/treatment. These will be used to structure the following section.

Week 1

Client contact

I began by providing students with opportunities to meet and relate with clients on an informal basis. For example, students attended home visits with therapists, who allowed time for informal discussions about the client's experience of the disability and occupational therapy.

Assessment and treatment

I began by exposing students to occupational therapy treatment using the same visits just discussed, but this aim was a secondary consideration. In addition, students accompanied therapists to treatment sessions and were encouraged to observe these sessions in an unfocused way.

Informal supervision took place after each visit, regardless of the purpose, in which students were encouraged to reflect upon what they had just seen. I would often ask students to reflect upon the *content* and *process* of sessions, the former being the information obtained which might be useful when considering occupational therapy interventions. Not only did this give students the chance to clarify procedural-type knowledge which they were unfamiliar with, it also meant they could begin refining their skills in distinguishing those aspects of the whole situation that were relevant and those that were not. The formal aspect of supervision drew very much on peer learning and student directedness. Students met together for one hour and discussed the week, highlighting any issues which had arisen, and compiled an agenda for a meeting with me. The meeting between the six of us began with agreeing an agenda which met both their needs to discuss certain issues and mine. During this first supervision session, the concept of learning contracts was introduced to students and they were encouraged to consider any individual learning needs they had and how these might be met during this placement. As the school of occupational therapy used learning contracts as the method of assessment for fieldwork education placements, this was an integral part of their placement.

Week 2

Client contact

Further opportunities were provided for students to meet people with disabilities but this time in non-health settings, so that students could begin to appreciate the lives of people with disabilities beyond the health service. In this case, students spent one day at a Social Services day centre for people with primarily physical disabilities. It was recognised, however, that the day centre was still exposing students to a view of people with disabilities within the health and social care sectors and that there were better settings. At the end of this day, students were asked to complete a reflective observation sheet which included the following sections.

1 People I met.
2 What I observed (including the purpose of interaction).
3 My initial reactions (what I thought and felt).
4 How did this relate to my past experiences?
5 What have I learnt from this experience?

This was the last week that specific sessions were organised for students to consider the illness experience of people with disabilities, but this continued to be a recurring theme throughout subsequent supervision sessions.

Assessment and treatment

Students observed assessment sessions and were provided with some way of structuring their thinking. For example, they usually attended initial assessments in pairs with one therapist. They were provided with the assessment form in advance and each student was asked to focus on only one section of the form. After the assessment was completed, students were asked to meet together and complete a full assessment form using the information both had obtained and this was then compared to the one completed by the therapist. Another method of structuring student observation was by asking one student to observe and comment on the process of the interview, while the other made notes on its content. During this week, each student also participated in a treatment session with a therapist with a view to taking over ongoing treatment with one client. Again, each session was followed by informal supervision with formal supervision at the end of each week.

Week 3

Assessment and treatment

During this week students were given the opportunity for safe practice of initial interviewing in the form of a role play with what I have come to call 'tag team' interviewing. I took on the role of a client I was familiar with while the students took it in turns to complete different aspects of an initial interview. At any time students were able to freeze the role play and either ask advice or discuss an issue with the other students or the second occupational therapist who was co-leading the session. At times, either my colleague or myself would freeze the role play to point out particular strengths or weaknesses or to ask students to justify their choice or consider alternatives. This entire session was recorded on video and left with students so they could watch the video either individually or with other students at a later time.

The next stage in this graded process, that was to culminate in students completing an initial interview independently, was conducting an initial interview jointly with one other student. This was completed with a therapist present and required one student to lead the initial interview with the other able to intervene and ask questions too. The leading student was able to ask the second student or the therapist for advice throughout or to hand the entire interview over, if necessary. Each student had the opportunity to lead one initial interview and to be co-assessor at one other. After this initial interview each student was required, with assistance from his/her partner if necessary, to devise an intervention plan for that client.

Students now had one client whom they were seeing regularly for ongoing treatment and this week they were required to conduct a treatment session devised by the therapist with supervision. Formal and informal supervision continued as in previous weeks.

Week 4

Assessment and treatment

During this week each student completed one initial interview independently with myself observing, after which they devised a treatment plan and began to implement it. Each student continued the ongoing treatment of at least one client, but this week began to take responsibility for treatment planning. Formal and informal supervision continued as in previous weeks.

Week 5

In this last week students continued with treatment implementation and conducted further initial interviews where possible and began to prepare for handing over their clients to members of staff. At the end of this week the formal assessments were completed, I provided each student with written and verbal feedback of his/her performance and each student completed a written evaluation of the placement.

LOOKING BACK

It has now been some time since that fieldwork placement, but I can still remember it and I am still committed to that model of fieldwork education. It gave me an opportunity to put into practice the knowledge I gained during the clinical reasoning module on my Masters degree and, to a lesser extent, that which I gained from the module on fieldwork education. In particular, my deeper understanding of clinical reasoning enabled me, on that placement and others, firstly to talk about my practice in a way I was unable to before. I can now describe the depth and breadth of practice with my new language of tacit knowledge, procedural, interactive, narrative images, the illness experience. Secondly, I am more in tune with the world of the novice and what aspects of clinical practice are more mysterious than others, which in turn allows me to structure situations and maximise learning.

On a lighter note, having the four students on placement with me using the programme was enjoyable. One of the benefits of taking students on placements is simply getting to meet new and different people and in this case I got to meet four people instead of one. The nature of the course they came from meant that each one was completely different not only in terms of personality but also in regard to their lives prior to commencing occupational therapy education – they were all interesting people. This uniqueness did have its unexpected challenges, however, the most significant being that it required me to constantly adapt my way of communicating with and thinking about each student. In a more traditional placement with one student, I would be able to familiarise myself with the particular ways in which that student thought about issues and learned most effectively. In this case, it was firstly more difficult to gain this knowledge from four people simultaneously but secondly, I needed to alter my approach depending on who I was speaking to at that point in time. In addition, having a small group of students gave me greater flexibility in designing learning opportunities. We could have group discussions, we could use role play, they could support each other in pairs and so on. Following the placement, Susan interviewed the students as a group (although only three were able to attend) and these transcripts have since been analysed to provide an insight into the students' experience of the placement.

I named the three themes which emerged as being a group, jumping in and a broadened perspective. The first theme, 'being a group', had a social component which included security, reassurance and will we get on? This was also related to the learning which took place and considered limited opportunities and working in pairs. Students reported that it felt very safe to be going on their first placement as a member of a group rather than an individual, almost natural, as they studied in groups while on the course. However, although the students had been working together as part of the whole cohort during the preplacement modules, they were not particularly familiar with each other as it was still quite early in their course. As a result a question which arose for many of them was 'Will we get on together?'. Another aspect of being part of a group was that it was very reassuring to have others in a similar situation around; they felt it minimised their anxiety.

In terms of the way the group impacted on learning, a significant initial concern for all the students was 'Would there be enough to go around?'. There seemed to be a real fear that they would not learn as much or see as much because there were other students with them. In retrospect, the students did not find these concerns to be entirely warranted and identified working in pairs for most of the placement to be a particular strength. They found it useful as it meant they could discuss issues with someone else who was their equal rather than having to discuss it with me all the time. It was also recognised that when interacting with clients, it was useful to watch their fellow student and examine their practice for tips and pointers. While this was the case when observing me and other therapists, it seemed there were some aspects of practice they saw in each other and not in myself or other therapists. A possible explanation for this is that for some students, a fellow student was closer to themselves on the novice–expert continuum than more experienced therapists were but at the same time might be slightly more advanced. The other student acted as an intermediary between them as the novice and me as the more experienced practitioner.

I named the second theme 'jumping in' as this captures the approach to the placement which students wished to take. The way the programme was structured meant that students had a very gradual introduction to working with clients. This began with free observation, then guided observation, opportunities for safe practice followed by more independent practice. Initially the students found this quite frustrating, as they had come on placement to work with clients so they felt they were being held back. After the placement they were able to appreciate the reasoning behind this graded approach and found it to be a useful model.

The final theme was related to the fact that students seemed to gain a broadened perspective of several dimensions of practice. First, they reported thinking quite critically about occupational therapy in a general sense. What are the skills of the profession? What is our true role? What are the potential opportunities? Second, they became very aware of various issues which impact on the delivery of occupational therapy services, such as staffing, funding and local relationships. Finally, as I had hoped, students did seem to gain a greater appreciation of the illness experience of clients rather than just the individual conditions. While one would hope that this occurs on traditional placements, on this placement specific opportunities were provided to enhance the development of this aspect of practice.

While all of those involved in this pilot were encouraged and excited by the results and our experience of the process, we acknowledge that more research is required to truly understand this type of fieldwork placement. Some ideas for future work include using this approach at different times throughout the curriculum, following students through coursework and placements which follow a similar design. To examine and attempt to track the development of student reasoning over a placement and a course would also prove invaluable.

THE JOURNEY CONTINUES

Through the experiences I have described and others that are beyond the scope of this chapter, I have come to believe very strongly that the understanding of clinical reasoning is an area which is absolutely fundamental to occupational therapy. I believe, therefore, that just as occupation should permeate all aspects of occupational therapy education, so too must clinical reasoning. It is insufficient to introduce students to clinical reasoning at the end of their education, just as it is inappropriate to teach clinical reasoning as a theoretical subject divorced from practice. To this end, I have designed, in conjunction with colleagues, a module which incorporates clinical reasoning into every session. Students are introduced to the concepts and models in the first week and subsequent weeks are devoted to working on client cases. Through these client cases, which are primarily paper based, students explore clinical reasoning alongside assessment methods, the occupational therapy process and particular conditions.

The use of narratives and stories has also had an impact on my current teaching outside the module I lead. One example is a session I was asked to lead on individual performance review/staff appraisal. Recognising this as a potentially dry session, I began to think of alternatives to overheads, definitions and lecturing. I decided to tell a story of a senior occupational therapist on my team in my last position. It was truly amazing to witness the change in students as I asked them to sit back and listen to a story. They all stopped writing, talking, looking out windows, whatever it was they were doing, and all eyes were fixed in silence on me as I told my story. Towards the end of my story I stopped and set them a task which they completed with enthusiasm before I finished the story. The discussions that took place during that session seemed so much richer than those in other sessions. I am sure it was because I was talking about a real person and because it was a *story*.

My interest in narratives, which has been developing since the module I completed on my Masters course, is now forming the basis of my PhD research. I will be collecting the individual life stories of people with HIV/AIDS and analysing these to explore the meaning of occupations in their lives and the pattern of engagement in occupation, before and after diagnosis. My research will contribute to ongoing work at the British Library National Sound Archive and I have listened to some of the histories already deposited there. As one would expect, they are riveting and rich with meaning. They are, after all, *stories*.

References

Brookfield, S. (1986) *Understanding and Facilitating Adult Learning*. Open University Press, Milton Keynes.

Fleming, M. (1991) The therapist with the three-track mind. *American Journal of Occupational Therapy*, 45(11), 1007–1014.

Mattingly, C. (1989) The narrative nature of clinical reasoning. Paper presented at a mini course in clinical reasoning, Annual Conference of the American Occupational Therapy Association, Baltimore (cited in Ryan, 1990).

Mattingly, C., Fleming, M. (1994) *Clinical Reasoning: Forms of Inquiry in a Therapeutic Practice*. F. A. Davis, Philadelphia.

Neistadt, M. (1987) Classroom as clinic: a model for teaching clinical reasoning in occupational therapy education. *American Journal of Occupational Therapy*, 41(10), 631–636.

Ryan, G. (1993) Student perceptions about self-directed learning in a professional course implementing problem-based learning. *Studies in Higher Education*, 18(1), 53–63.

Ryan, S. (1990) Clinical reasoning: a descriptive study comparing novice and experienced occupational therapists. Unpublished Masters thesis, Columbia University, New York.

School of Occupational Therapy (1995) Submission for the validation of a Diploma of Occupational Therapy to be awarded by the University of London. School of Occupational Therapy, London Hospital Medical College, London.

10 STUDENTS' FIELDWORK STORIES: REFLECTING ON SUPERVISION

Tracy Fortune

KEY POINTS
- Undergraduate and postgraduate education
- Facilitating story sharing and story making
- Supervision enhancing fieldwork
- Working creatively

Here, the author explores the usefulness of fieldwork supervision to first- and third-year students. She highlights the need for the fieldwork supervisors to be proactive in sharing their narratives which enables students to tease out the complexity of their clients' life stories. The need for this information to be tailored to the student's level of understanding and experience is paramount. Discussion of such stories should focus on the unpredictable facets which could have many interpretations and resultant treatment interventions.

This chapter is concerned with exploring and illuminating the role of reflective learning in the education and professional development of both undergraduate and graduate therapists. In some respects, what is to follow may appear as an analysis of some of my own observations and concerns regarding how reflective fieldwork supervision actually is. It is likely that you will observe this through the literature I choose to incorporate and the numerous questions I pose. These questions do reflect some of my own struggles with what I have observed throughout my roles as supervising therapist and now as a participant in the fieldwork education of undergraduate students. Among the many questions are: what stories can supervising therapists share . . . and in what ways can they assist those who seek their guidance, towards a co-creation of new therapeutic stories? Are learners encouraged to share their thinking and is there an opportunity to transform past stories into new chapters of doing and being which is, arguably, the goal towards which many therapists work?

Within the field of occupational therapy, the movement of students towards becoming creative and artistic practitioners depends on the adoption of many of the ideals related to self-directed learning (Boud, 1988). Some of the key concepts of such an orientation to learning include the facilitation of critical enquiry and reflective analysis skills. In the practice professions where university based students are expected to complete fieldwork, the enhancement of critical enquiry and reflective skills may, to some extent, be dependent on an explicit acknowledgment by fieldwork educators (practitioners) of the reasoning surrounding their own client related practical action. Do students see reflection and critical enquiry, modelled by therapists in the field?

Occupational therapists could be described as meaning makers (Mattingly and Fleming, 1994), or artistic directors, who provide opportunities for people to plot out their own life narrative in the face of challenges to 'doing' and 'being'. Thus, as a practice occupational therapy is concerned with the ability of people to 'function' at a self-determined level and to be seen by society as occupying a valued role(s). Implicit in the challenge to assist people towards a certain functional level and valued social role is a need to ascertain people's own version of what they want to do and be. The question of how therapists learn to listen for stories, retell and remake life stories is an interesting one. Is it impossible at an undergraduate level? Do we have to wait until therapists are 'qualified' before we start examining and teaching this fine art of therapeutic story making and telling? Do those charged with developing the therapeutic competence of learners think in terms of stories? Perhaps students and seasoned therapists are uncomfortable with the use of a story analogy as they struggle in their efforts to appear 'scientific'. But perhaps for learning and professional growth, our words must begin to speak as loudly as our actions. What are the words of our clients? How do we transform their actions and words in our minds and what outlets exist to recreate, cut, paste and edit?

This chapter is not particularly concerned with the development of technical skills for precise application. Rather, it will focus on how students and developing therapists can be facilitated in their professional development to create meaningful wholes from uncertain and ill-defined scenarios, context constraints and challenging sociocultural environments. These are, after all, the backdrops against which many human occupations are enacted. The metaphor of storytelling in both a verbal or action sense is felt to be an appropriate one for occupational therapy (Mattingly and Fleming, 1994). The idea is implied that in order to *direct* one must have opportunities to *reflect*. The notion of the therapist as a director is offered not in an authoritarian, but in a facilitatory sense. In a similar manner to a film director working with an actor, an occupational therapist frames scenes that allow a client to perform in a way best suited to the story which they hope to bring life to.

Undergraduate students with varying levels of experience in the fieldwork learning environment will share their experiences of how they have been encouraged to reflect and share stories. From the author's perspective, enquiry and subsequent interpretation of 'narrative' data collected from these learners are explicitly focused on delving into the reflective nature of supervision. Practically, it will also focus on what potentials exist for the inclusion of more reflective learning opportunities within the parameters of what may be regular, or quite irregular and informal supervision. These potential learning opportunities are assumed to be those which develop 'artistically oriented' enquiry skills which can be drawn on in a variety of divergent situations, rather than those techniques of practical teaching which seek to provide direct instruction in technical application skills in specific and known situations. Such situations, it could be argued, tend to rely on the facilitation of a more procedural type of reasoning (Fleming, 1991) and are characteristic of vocation training courses or technician training. It is my view that occupational therapy education has moved beyond the realm of technical application of tried and true procedures, in an effort to consider more complex philosophical, moral, environmental, social and cultural determinants of occupational dysfunction at both a community and individual level.

REFLECTION: THINKING BACK IN ORDER TO MOVE AHEAD!

Schon's (1983, 1987) work relating to the development of reflective practice amongst academically educated practitioners is well known. Although Schon spoke most explicitly of reflection-in-action (1987), I am more concerned with reflection-on-action and specifically how developing therapists can learn through revisiting actions/experiences and their own thoughts surrounding these. Within a story analogy, this involves telling or reconstructing the story of a client who has been observed or actively engaged in therapy (Mattingly and Fleming, 1994). Reflection-in-action whilst more immediately experientially related, will be assumed, due to the many context constraints on supervisors, to be difficult to engage in. The author, following many discussions with fieldwork supervisors, assumes this difficulty. These supervisors explain that due to the solitary nature of their work and the multiple role commitments within either interdisciplinary or multidisciplinary teams, they are hard pressed to provide direct in-action supervision or coaching, as Schon calls it (1987). Further, increasing use of non-traditional or 'project' type fieldwork experiences (Fortune and Adamson, 1997), which do not utilise as their primary supervision model practitioners from the same discipline as the learner, call for new models of learning through reflection-on-action, in which the learner is required to adopt a self-directed approach.

Schon (1987) provides us with an insight into the type of learning environment the 'practicum' could become, when he contrasts the traditional practicum model with one which conjures up images of a messy 'think tank', where learners and supervisors jointly explore, share and construct meaning from past events. Schon describes the traditional fieldwork learning scenario as follows:

> *In simulated, partial, or protected form, they engage in the practice they wish to learn . . . They do these things under the guidance of a senior practitioner . . . a studio master, a supervising physician or case instructor. From time to time these individuals teach in the conventional sense, communicating information, advocating theories, describing examples of practice. Mainly, however, they function as coaches whose main activities are demonstrating, advising, questioning and criticising. (p. 38)*

In describing a step beyond this model, which focuses on the development of professional 'knowing', Schon explains that:

> *. . . students will still learn relevant facts and operations but will also learn the forms of enquiry by which competent practitioners reason their way in*

problematic instances, to clear connections between general knowledge and particular cases. (p. 39)

In a third stage of 'practicum' students are encouraged to devise their own reasoning methods and problem action approaches. In such an orientation to practical learning, Schon tells us, 'Coaches will emphasise indeterminate zones of practice and reflective conversations with the materials of the situation' (p. 40). This approach also allows for mutual learning, where both learner and supervisor stand to develop new insights into their own reasoning and practice behaviour.

It is not advocated that a traditional approach to practical supervision be totally abandoned, but that new considerations are given to a more deeply reflective approach. In such an approach, the transmission of facts and techniques and the application of procedural schedules of enquiry are balanced equally with an open and reflective dialogue. Such an approach is hinted at by a number of authors. A dialectical mode which uses reflection to transform practice is discussed by Wellington and Austin (1996), who believe that such an approach, through reconstruction of experience, can facilitate political and personal liberation. Self-determination in thinking on an equal level with freedom to express divergent reasoning styles, which may not fit with the standard schedules of enquiry, may allow liberation for both supervisor and learner. Authenticity, a term offered by Webb (1995), is viewed in a similar vein but from the viewpoint of the supervisor or 'staff developer' where an openness between learner and 'staff developer' can enhance learning for both. The:

> *... staff developer's task is to identify his or her own prejudices and to hold them open to query within the staff development conversation. As we seek to understand others, there is always the possibility of a 'fusion of horizons' which enlarges our own position. (p. 75)*

Both the learner and supervisor may relate one crucial concern with such approaches to a level of discomfort. On the one hand, students may see reflective learning practices as a waste of time, being desperate to pick up the technical nuts and bolts of the situation. Schon describes a source of resistance to the development of artistry through reflection:

> *... the mood of vocationalism and consumerism among students in the professional school – so easily translatable into a thirst for the 'hard skills' embodied in sophisticated techniques. (p. 313)*

My own anecdotal observations inform me that learners in earlier years of undergraduate programmes may feel discomfort with educators who clearly convey the 'muddiness' of a situation or choose not to (or realistically cannot) provide a concrete solution or response when one may well not be at hand. These observations also tell me that those students close to graduation appear more comfortable with the 'fuzziness' of reality, despite being somewhat daunted by the prospect of soon having to engage with it on a daily basis.

Learners may also be terrified to offer their own theories or true reasoning for fear of being criticised or marked unfairly on their fieldwork assessment. Examples of this might involve the suppression of felt emotions, perhaps stirred through experiences with clients who might appear hostile or ungrateful (Carson, 1997). Can learners feel safe to explain their feelings of anger towards certain individuals in the practical situation, or is it better to gloss over such reactions during the supervision session, in an effort to appear that the adoption of a professional tolerance has been attained? In relaying what appears to be a crucial realisation of the 'muddiness' of occupational therapy practice, a participant in Deveny's (1997) enquiry into the third-year fieldwork learning experience reveals:

This placement has made me realise that, with some clients, meaningful activity is not really possible. I'd get killed for saying that, but with some of my clients, I just can't do it. (p. 89)

What learning opportunities are lost when neither learner nor supervisor can share mutual experiences and construct ways forward as a result of such realisations?

Similarly, supervisors may themselves be very uncomfortable with the idea of sharing thoughts, theories and reasonings related to their own practice. Whilst actively advocating the use of procedural schedules and pointing out the correct way, in an effort to maintain a professional and/or scientific approach, the supervisor may be denying their own artistry, their own ability to reason through very complex situations in unconventional though highly effective ways. Can supervising practitioners comfortably make the transition towards being 'sharers' of uncertainty? Schon's distinctions between how 'experts' as opposed to 'reflective practitioners' (1983) view their clients can be readily translated to fit the learner–supervisor relationship. In applying this thinking, the supervisor as reflective practitioner would recognise that within such a relationship they are 'not the only one in the situation to have relevant and important knowledge. My uncertainties may be a source of learning for me and them' and allow 'respect for my knowledge to emerge from their discovery of it in the situation'. Finally, the reflective practitioner would 'look for the sense of freedom and of real connection as a consequence of no longer needing to maintain a professional facade' (p. 300).

STORIES FROM THE FIELD: HOW REFLECTIVE IS SUPERVISION?

The above question formed the basis for a formal enquiry into some of my own concerns and others suggested to me through literature.

Gathering stories: how I went about it

Questionnaires requiring written open-ended feedback were distributed to all first- and third-year occupational therapy students of Charles Sturt University. Both year levels had just returned from the field, with the former having completed three weeks and the latter, nine weeks.

The questionnaires sought to ascertain how reflective students perceived their supervision to be and, specifically, for them to describe:

- how they were facilitated as learners to explore their observations, actions and emerging clinical reasoning;
- situations of joint or mutual exploration of actions or reasoning (sharing thinking).

Questionnaire completion was voluntary and no names were sought but students were asked to state their year level. Each question requested a response of some 5–10 lines or one to two paragraphs.

Participants' responses were analysed in their entirety in relation to each question. I cued into descriptions which I felt were conveying a 'story' of supervision and, more specifically, which offered a potential insight into supervisory practice which appears to support learning through reflection or otherwise.

Stories from third-year students

The third-year practicum is for these participants the first extended period in the field. They are expected to begin practising assessment and treatment skills with increasing levels of autonomy as the nine weeks progress. In most instances, these students have a period of observation where expected assessment and treatment behaviours are modelled, with varying levels of participation being offered. After this time, students are allocated 'cases' which are theirs to manage and work through with varying degrees of supervision. The following stories talk about a number of facets of this 'supervision'.

Supervision: formal or informal?

The majority of students who replied to the questionnaire described a predominantly informal approach to supervision, where supervisor and student caught up as and when needed according to both their schedules. Several students described that their supervision was formal in the initial weeks and then tapered off to informal in the final week. Two students only described a separate set time for formal supervision on a weekly basis in addition to informal supervision.

Meetings weekly with a clinical coordinator was an opportunity to meet with someone not (directly) involved in supervision and time to reflect on highlights of the week.

Another describes a style of supervision which appears to promote enquiry and reflection, through going back over past actions.

Informal supervision was facilitated by (my) supervisor enquiring about my thoughts of a particular observation, my rationale behind a particular practice (assessment, treatment aims) and particular frame of reference. It was facilitated by more of a discussion/feedback of a session I facilitated.

Being facilitated to share and reflect

The following stories speak about the issue of joint reflection. There appears to be a continuum at play whereby some supervision relationships actively encourage and are composed of both reflection and equal sharing of those reflections. This differs from those relationships which could appear less supportive of learning through reflection in addition to being very unequal in terms of sharing of reasoning and acknowledgment of the complexity of practice.

> *I was asked how I felt about a session, what I felt was good and bad. I was asked how I felt before and during and what was it that made me feel this way. It was really good to hear how my supervisor felt throughout the session. She said that in one session she felt totally out of depth and really struggled with one particular client. This was really good to hear as you don't feel like you're the only one that is unsure. It seemed to create a closer working relationship and a shared role in therapy sessions.*

> *Whenever I asked a question my supervisor would always turn it back on me and say, 'well, what do you think?'. She never expressed her own thoughts and opinions directly and certainly never shared her own experiences.*

> *I found I tended to offer my thoughts rather than being encouraged/asked to share them by my supervisor. My supervisor did express her thoughts but again, often I had to ask her to share them.*

Moving beyond procedural reasoning

Students were asked to consider the values they felt that their supervisors placed on reasoning about situations in certain ways. Implicit in the researcher's posing of this question was an idea that some supervising therapists may place differing emphasis on the relative importance of interactive, subjective or non-procedural ways of learning, when compared to a more procedural way of knowing. Do supervising therapists facilitate students to think about the grey areas of practice as they arise?

> *The focus during supervision was more with technical and diagnostic aspects of reasoning. It focused on how to do things and why these things should be done. However, answers to 'why' were often very vague. For example, when I asked why the OT treated arms and not legs to increase range of movement and normalise muscle tone, the answer was that 'this was the way we have always done it here'.*

Such a response is particularly telling. In many ways it suggests to us that supervising therapists do not question their role and the scope of occupational therapy and that students are not encouraged to do this either. In effect, the grey zones of practice are not up for critical analysis or, if they are, are not felt to be appropriate for students to grapple with. We may consider this to be somewhat disheartening if we subscribe to the view that fieldwork learning is the key arena for students to work through the question 'What is occupational therapy?'. Another student explains:

The majority of the focus was on technical and diagnostic aspects of OT . . . I believe that learning diagnostic aspects is very important but also very easily learned. However, other factors are more difficult to grapple with and I would have liked to have gone into greater depth about it.

Here we receive a hint of the potential value of reflection-on-action, in recognition of the fact that there are some situations that defy understanding, even with adequate theoretical preparation.

Finally, one student talks about 'strategies' and being implicitly encouraged to try these out in difficult situations which pose moral dilemmas for learners.

One client . . . very upper-middle class . . . I would be infuriated by the manner she treated the domestic staff, particularly those who had English as a second language, I found it embarrassing and rude. Several times I discussed this with my supervisor . . . this was appropriate because one of my clients was offending me . . . and we would discuss strategies to deal with it . . . being able to discuss the issue was important as it demonstrated that I wasn't the first person to come across someone I didn't like.

Enhancement of practical learning

Students were asked to offer their suggestions for how learning could be improved during their fieldwork experience.

Although I was given a balance between informal and formal supervision, I felt I needed to chase specific feedback. Not until my mid-week review did I know how my supervisor thought I was doing. By being left in the dark, I felt unsure as to whether I was on the right track, meeting expectations. I do not feel that it is the student's responsibility to be 'chasing' feedback continuously. It can affect a student's confidence and subsequent performance. Further, supervision could have been improved if provided with different outlooks on ways of providing services or possible avenues to explore.

Discussions before and after sessions (especially at the beginning of placement) . . . given opportunity to show initiative and demonstrate knowledge . . . given time to reflect, think how things could have been done differently. By feedback [I mean] . . . opportunity to observe others . . . [to be] challenged on thinking and opinions being sought and treated as valid.

For supervisors to be more reflective and discuss how they would do things and how they would react in certain situations. This would give the student a role model so that appropriate professional behaviours could be modelled.

The value of reflection, non-procedural reasoning and more formal opportunities to extend thinking in relation to fieldwork experiences is highlighted in various ways through these students' words.

Stories from first-year students

The focus of the first-year fieldwork practicum is to provide a largely observational experience whereby students receive an introduction to the culture of the occupational therapy profession. With the focus of learning less on 'doing' and more on watching, listening and asking or carrying out aspects of assessment or treatment under close supervision, a valuable reflective learning situation may be hypothesised. Again, these stories speak for themselves as first years candidly offer their opinions on the learning opportunities they were exposed to.

Being facilitated to share and reflect

My first supervisor wasn't very talkative, so I found it very difficult to gain her opinions. I found that by reading her reports in files I could obtain knowledge of how she thought. My second supervisor was much better. We openly discussed issues, opinions and plans of action. I learned a great deal more from this as one is able to retain more information when told rather than reading text.

Enhancement of practical learning

I was very lucky with my supervisor. She gave me constant feedback on her own thoughts and impressions and also came back to tell me when she was found to be wrong. As a first-year student, I was a bit hesitant to put forward too many of my own opinions and I felt quite uncomfortable with this (there's no point being shot down in flames).

I thought it was great after each session to be asked what I thought and then to have a discussion with my supervisor's thoughts and reflections as well. I was able to identify what I thought and when we discussed our ideas, I was able to reflect on my ideas clearly with someone else's opinion to help me make my ideas more relative, to see what other people thought.

My placement was sometimes primarily observation but I still managed to discuss my observation with the therapist which helped my learning.

My supervisor shared her own feelings often when I expressed mine. She was also able to relate my experience to when she was in university placements which really helped me. I gained a lot more confidence by sharing my feelings and thoughts as I received a lot of positive feedback by doing so. I found my feelings/ thoughts were usually what my supervisor was also feeling or has felt in a similar situation so I didn't feel so silly.

I was always encouraged to share my thoughts and feelings on what I had observed. The supervisors were always willing to listen and tell me what they felt about what they had observed. Being able to express my own thoughts and feelings gave me confidence and enabled me to reflect on what I had experienced. It was also a good way to get feedback as to whether I was on the right track. If the supervisor was concerned about something they told me in a nice way . . . I think feedback sessions with supervisors really enhance learning and reflection. You learn so much from just discussing what you just observed, your thoughts and listening to the supervisor's thoughts.

This final section of opinions from first years is particularly telling. These students describe highly positive learning experiences based on reflection and the sharing of these.

PROMOTING REFLECTIVE SUPERVISION: LEARNING FROM LEARNERS

Students clearly value opportunities to discuss ideas openly, to offer ideas without 'being shot down in flames' and to have some validation that they are on the right track. First-year student transcripts in particular highlight the type of learning environment and supervisory actions that promote learning through reflection, whether this be a learning experience that took the form of an enacted therapy task or the observation of such.

Students appear to greatly value the exposure to role models but it is clear that this value goes beyond the idea of modelling therapeutic actions. Students also highly value the modelling of reasoning and thinking out aloud, of questioning oneself and one's profession. Perhaps such actions or modes of supervision are, for first years, particularly enculturating. As such, the first-year supervisor may be conveying a message along the lines of 'Welcome to this practice of unknowns, where you and I will continue to learn together throughout our careers'.

It is also possible that the greater focus on positive reflective experiences highlighted by first years in comparison to third years may be a consequence of the focus on how and what students are expected to learn at these different levels. Third-year students are expected to practise the actions of a therapist and to be seen to be competent in these. First-year students, on the other hand, are expected to demonstrate that they have some appreciation of the scope of the profession in a very broad sense. Part of gaining personal clarity on this necessitates discussion and a struggle with trying to 'fit' observations and experiences with a minimal amount of theory. It appears that the brief of the placement gives both first-year student and supervisor 'permission' to be highly reflective.

Later year placements may, on the other hand, through their focus on having to get down to the actions of therapy, not so readily provide this permission to either student or supervisor. If this is in fact a possibility, there are implications for learning not only amongst these students but also amongst new graduate or beginner therapists and particularly those who have access to minimal supervision.

So what can be done? I believe that the first-year transcripts provide many hints for action. Both students and new graduate therapists must begin their careers with an orientation to learning that promotes and values what they can learn through reflecting on experiences with supervisors. Students should also be exposed early in their learning to the complexities and 'muddiness' of practice, either through working directly with clients who have complex life stories or through exposure to the actions and thinking of their supervisors surrounding such practice situations. The ability to learn through reflection requires a commitment to the retelling of stories. Students and supervisors need to listen out for and reflect on these stories which relay the grey areas This sharing of grey narratives should enable both students and therapists to create meaningful interventions which could open up to their clients the possibilities of constructing new life stories.

Further thoughts

---

1 During practice, take time to compare and contrast your story of a client with your supervisor's story, so that you can compare and contrast the similarities and differences of your reasoning and reflections.
2 As a fieldwork supervisor, consider the ways in which you can make explicit, to students or newly graduated therapists, your reasoning and ways of working with a specific client at any one time. In what ways could you check out the student's understanding of your explanation?
3 As a fieldwork supervisor, what opportunities do you provide for students to expand their reasoning?

REFERENCES

Boud, D. (ed.) (1988) *Developing Student Autonomy in Learning*, 2nd edn. Kogan Page, London.
Carson, T. (1997) The student experience of working with people who are dying. In T. Fortune and L. Adamson (eds) *Occupational Therapy at Charles Sturt University: The First Four Years*. Charles Sturt University, Albury.
Deveny, H. (1997) Third year fieldwork through the eyes of students: expectations, preparation and challenges to ideas of occupational therapy. In T. Fortune and L. Adamson (eds) *Occupational Therapy at Charles Sturt University: The First Four Years*. Charles Sturt University, Albury.
Fleming, M. (1991) The therapist with the three-track mind. *American Journal of Occupational Therapy*, 45(11), 1007–1041.
Fortune, T., Adamson, L. (eds) (1997) Fieldwork education. In *Occupational Therapy at Charles Sturt University: The First Four Years*. Charles Sturt University, Albury.
Mattingly, C., Fleming, M. H. (1994) *Clinical Reasoning: Forms of Inquiry in a Therapeutic Practice*. F. A. Davis, Philadelphia.
Schon, D. (1983) *The Reflective Practitioner*. Basic Books, New York.
Schon, D. (1987) *Educating the Reflective Practitioner*. Jossey-Bass, San Francisco.
Wellington, B., Austin, P. (1996) Orientations to reflective practice. *Educational Research*, 38, 307–315.
Webb, G. (1995) Reflective practice, staff development and understanding. *Studies in Continuing Education*, 17, 70–77.

Index _____